GEORGIA O'KEEFFE

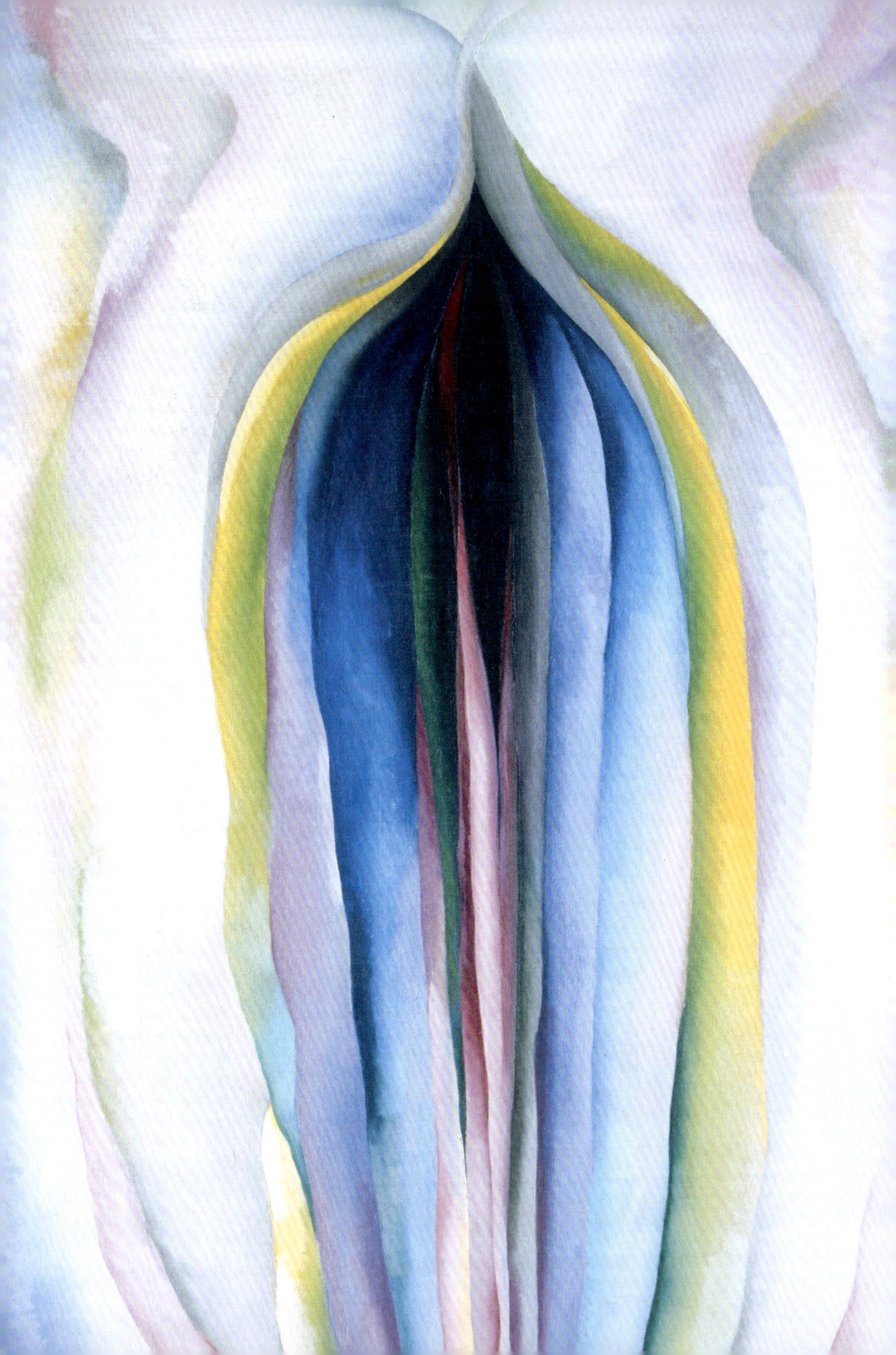

GEORGIA O'KEEFFE

GENEVIEVE BARTON

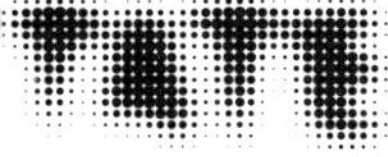

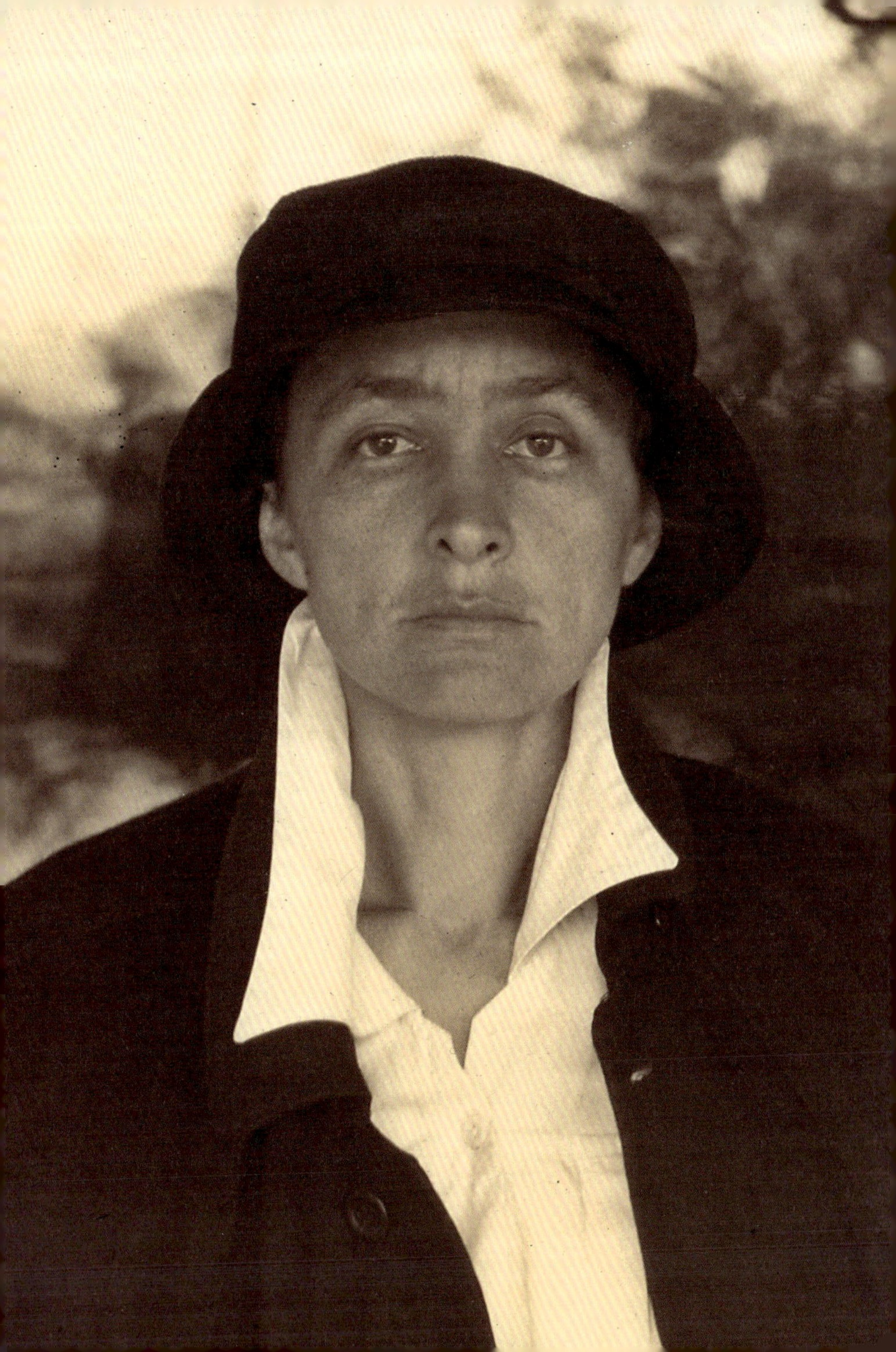

Georgia O'Keeffe has come to be known as one of the most celebrated American modernist painters of the twentieth century. Spanning over six decades, her career was defined by an independent spirit, a penetrating vision, and a magnetic appeal that traversed genres and generations. Change was a guiding principle for O'Keeffe, and the thousands of artworks she produced during her lifetime speak to her unblinking commitment to an evolution of self-expression and artistic development.

For O'Keeffe, art begins in the natural world. Concurrently, she saw art as a disciplined practice that connects us to a spiritual understanding, drawing inspiration from Buddhist tradition. She is well known for her paintings of flowers and bones, the New York City skyline and Southwest landscapes, and for her relationship with the pre-eminent photographer, collector and gallerist Alfred Stieglitz.

Just as O'Keeffe resisted straightforward definitions of her private selfhood, her artistic identity was equally ambiguous. She defied traditional power structures and ways of living, instead constructing a life replete with nerve, autonomy and new experiences. A role model for creative freedom and societal liberation, revered and imitated by countless artists, O'Keeffe carved out a distinct individual aesthetic by striving to make 'the unknown – known'.[1] She was deeply affected by her surroundings and the natural world, while working from a place of 'inner harmony'.[2] Yet the mysteries of the enigmatic painter continue to be uncovered as scholars, writers, artists and poets reach further into her artistic practice and personal archive. Her cultural impact extends from a 1939 fruit company campaign to 1970s second-wave feminism, TV shows, recent immersive art experiences and, most significantly, her influence on a younger generation of artists.

EARLY YEARS

Born on 15 November 1887 to Frank and Ida O'Keeffe, Georgia Totto O'Keeffe grew up in the vast Midwestern region of prairies and far-reaching farmland. In the mid-nineteenth century, her home state of Wisconsin was divided into geometric parcels of land. Her father farmed the land, and her mother presided over the domestic realm. Ida was an intelligent and fiercely independent woman who instilled in Georgia a love of books and art, yet seldom provided the maternal warmth and comfort Georgia craved.

Alfred Stieglitz
Georgia O'Keeffe 1921
Photograph, gelatin silver print on paper

O'Keeffe enjoyed her own company and spent much of her childhood drawing and playing in the garden. As the eldest daughter of seven children, she was afforded a level of privacy and independence. Given a room of her own, she held a unique and authoritative position within the family.[3] She attended Sacred Heart Academy, a boarding school in Wisconsin, where she was liked by her fellow students and her talent was noticed early on, which was subsequently nurtured through private drawing lessons. Observant and precocious as a child, O'Keeffe often asked pertinent questions of her teachers. By the age of twelve, she had already declared her ambition to be an artist.

In 1902 her family relocated to Virginia, living at Wheatlands House where the children roamed freely on nine acres of land. O'Keeffe continued to board in Wisconsin, joining her family permanently in 1903. At the age of eighteen, she secured a place at the prestigious School of the Art Institute of Chicago, where she was taught by the Dutch American artist John Vanderpoel in the academic European manner. Although conservative and rigorous in its traditional training, at the institute O'Keeffe learned the principles of drawing from plaster casts and life models, providing her with the skills that would benefit her future career. Her schooling, however, was cut short in the summer of 1906 when she contracted typhoid fever and returned to the family home in Williamsburg.

After several tormenting months when her hair fell out, she eventually recovered, in preparation for her enrolment at the Art Students League in New York in autumn 1907. Here, O'Keeffe experienced for the first time complete independence from her relatives and with her newfound freedom, living at a young women's boarding house, she immersed herself in the New York art scene. The city offered abundant opportunities for new experiences and an alternative art education. Taught by European-trained painter William Merritt Chase she honed her skills in academic draughtsmanship. In 1908 she won the Chase Summer School scholarship for her painting *Dead Rabbit and Copper Pot*. The moody tones and inventive composition, distinctly different from the flat planes and bold colours of her later work, were highly regarded by her teachers and peers. Without financial support from her parents, she travelled back to Chicago in autumn 1908 to make a living as a commercial illustrator.

RADICAL ABSTRACTIONS: A CATALYST FOR CHANGE

In 1912, O'Keeffe began studying under Alon Bement at the University of Virginia. Through his classes she encountered the progressive system of thought proffered by American painter Arthur Wesley Dow. Renowned for his experimental design theories, Dow had a considerable impact on young artists in the first decades of the twentieth century. He was a proponent of Japanese techniques, drawing inspiration from the concept of *notan* (light and dark tonal contrasts) and the stylised designs of ukiyo-e prints.[4] Originally published in 1899, *Composition: A Series of Exercises in Art Structure for the Use of Students and Teachers*, Dow's highly significant text, was a guiding tome for American art students. His teachings radically altered the way young artists thought about and produced work, successfully fostering an equal appreciation of the many different art forms including painting, printmaking, ceramics, design and photography. In 1914–15, O'Keeffe studied with Dow at Columbia University's Teachers College, New York, which had a lasting impact. During this formative time, she met Anita Pollitzer and despite their age difference (Pollitzer was seven years younger than O'Keeffe), the pair became close friends. Pollitzer was an avid reader of political texts and poetry, and introduced O'Keeffe to the women's liberation movement. O'Keeffe also subscribed to the radical socialist journal, *The Masses* (1911–17), and was steadily involved in political activity for the first years of her early adulthood, becoming a member of the National Woman's Party in 1914, although later stepping away from immediate engagement.

The year 1915 was pivotal for O'Keeffe. After months spent teaching in Texas and Virginia and studying in New York, she began a position as an art tutor at Columbia College, South Carolina. This provided a regular income for the artist and allowed her to paint and draw often. The letters sent to and received from Pollitzer throughout this period were the connecting thread to her previous New York life. Inspired by Dow's teaching, O'Keeffe took a new instinctual direction, working monochromatically, and began a series of radical abstractions in charcoal. In December 1915, O'Keeffe wrote to Pollitzer of her breakthrough: 'Did you ever have something to say and feel as if the whole side of the wall wouldn't be big enough to say it on and then sit down on the floor and try to get it on to a sheet of charcoal paper [sic]'.[5] With the letter, she enclosed a selection of charcoal drawings with strict

Early Abstraction 1915
Charcoal on paper
61 × 47.3

instructions not to show them to anyone. Ignoring O'Keeffe's wishes, on 1 January 1916 Pollitzer took them directly to Alfred Stieglitz of '291' gallery in New York.[6] *The Specials*, as O'Keeffe titled them, were innovatively abstract works unique to O'Keeffe's idiosyncratic vision consisting of shapes emulating the natural world; the drawings were evocations of the artist's inner feelings (pp.26–7). Influenced by Japanese and Chinese painting and calligraphy, she worked through new ideas in mark making. Stieglitz was immediately struck by their singular style and forceful presence. Pollitzer wrote back informing O'Keeffe of Stieglitz's enthusiasm and his plans to show them at 291. Encouraged and uplifted by his admiration for her work, O'Keeffe continued to produce charcoal experiments for the next few months (p.28). In May 1916, Stieglitz organised an exhibition of ten of O'Keeffe's drawings without her prior permission, alongside works by American artists Charles Duncan and René Lafferty. At first disgruntled by his audacity, she soon struck up correspondence with Stieglitz, the leading advocate for American modernist art, later expressing in July 1916 that the drawings were 'as much yours as mine'.[7]

These early drawings echo the forms and shapes that photographers were investigating at the turn of the twentieth century. The young American photographer Paul Strand, ensconced into Stieglitz's inner circle around 1912, initially followed in the vein of the pictorialists who sought to position photography as a fine art. He began a more modernist style from 1915, constructing abstractions by closely cropping and flattening everyday landscapes and objects into simplified forms and patterns. In this manner, Strand and O'Keeffe shared a similar outlook. As curator Sarah Greenough has noted, O'Keeffe was 'fascinated with the way in which photography articulated not only shape, but [also] form'.[8] In March 1916, Stieglitz mounted an exhibition of Strand's new body of work titled *Photographs of New York and Other Places* at 291. In Spring 1916, O'Keeffe returned to New York to attend further classes with Dow, and may well have visited Strand's show. Moreover, by then, O'Keeffe was an avid reader of *Camera Work* (1903–17), Stieglitz's influential avant-garde photographic quarterly, which Pollitzer sent to her while she was in South Carolina, and O'Keeffe would have seen the work of Strand, and other photographers, reproduced in the publications.

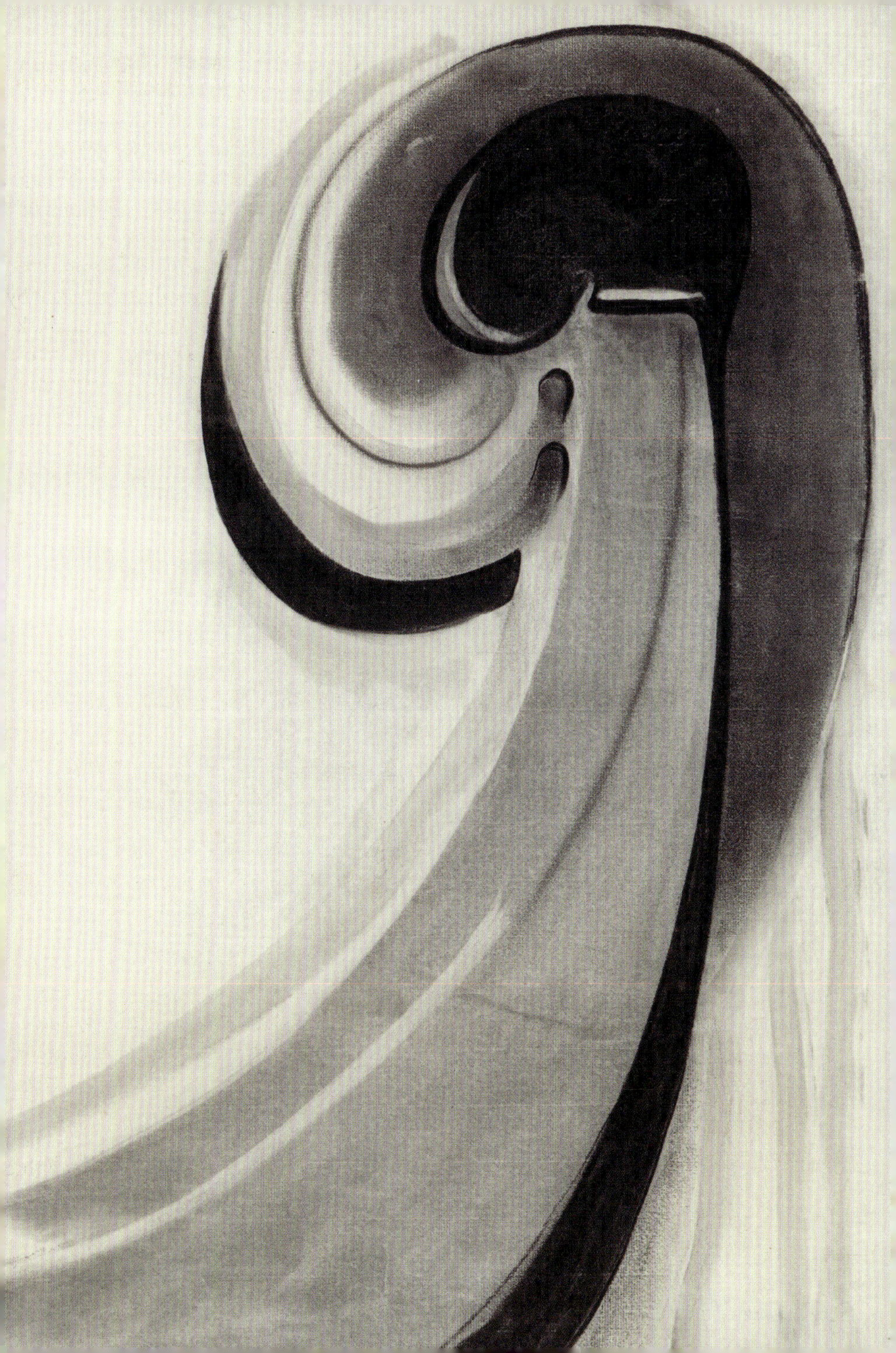

MUSIC

Music was a continual source of deep pleasure and creative sustenance for O'Keeffe. Her interest stemmed from her early accomplishments learning the piano and violin as a child. Innately curious, she wished to express 'a feeling like wonderful music gives me'.[9] O'Keeffe encountered the writing of the Russian artist Wassily Kandinsky, which Stieglitz had reproduced in *Camera Work* in 1912, finding connection in his treatise *Concerning the Spiritual in Art* (1911, translated to English in 1914). In this theoretical work, Kandinsky underscored the

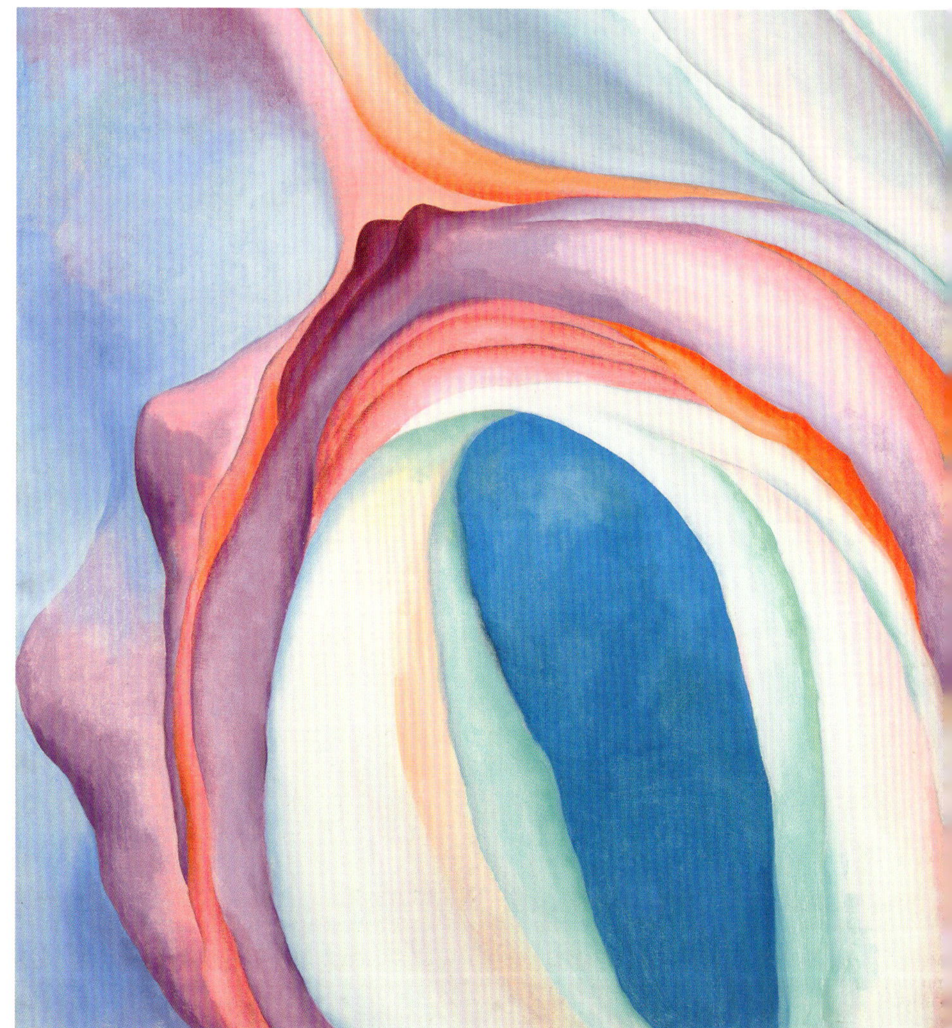

importance of questioning the seemingly rigid boundaries between the different creative mediums. Interested in the neurodiverse condition of synaesthesia – when a person experiences one sense through another – he encouraged artists to experiment with the vital interconnectedness of form and colour.

Music, Pink and Blue No. 2 1918 (opposite) demonstrates O'Keeffe's deep affinity to music. Through Kandinsky's text, and her conversations with Stieglitz (he wrote to her that her solo exhibition at 291 had 'a feeling of space – a great beautiful livingness and an unspeakable *fineness* – like string music – clear & crisp'[10]), she believed art could communicate the inner truth of emotions. As curator Lisa Mintz Messinger has observed, the music paintings 'gently ripple with movement'.[11] The diaphanous arches of soft pinks, purples and whites evoke the soaring sensation of musical compositions, the shapes engendering a synergy between the two art forms.

EARLY WATERCOLOURS

In September 1916, O'Keeffe was offered a prestigious teaching position as head of the art department at a school in Canyon, Texas. While there, she began working feverishly in watercolour, creating tender and surprising paintings (pp. 30–1). She fell for the grandeur of the landscape, integrating it into her small-scale watercolour works. Writing to Stieglitz on 4 September 1916, she poetically and emphatically expressed her love for her surroundings: 'The plains – the wonderful great big sky – makes me want to breathe so deep that I'll break – There is so much of it – I want to get outside of it all – I would if I could – even if it killed me.'[12]

Cosmic Cities, Grand Canyon of Arizona, painted by Dow in 1912, uses light, shape and tone to create a symphony of colour that mystically dances into the distance. Much of O'Keeffe's work after her return to colour in 1916 emulated Dow's style, committing to his ethos of harmonious and balanced compositions. Five years after Dow painted *Cosmic Cities*, O'Keeffe produced a series of watercolour landscapes that exploit this notion of harmony and balance. One such watercolour was *Canyon with Crows* 1917 (p.12), whereby the artist demonstrates the same striking use of light, shape and tone. The expressionistically vivid colours, even in the usually tempered medium of watercolour, fluidly capture the expert understanding of balance of form. Made the same year were

Music, Pink and Blue No.2
1918
Oil paint on canvas
88.9 × 76

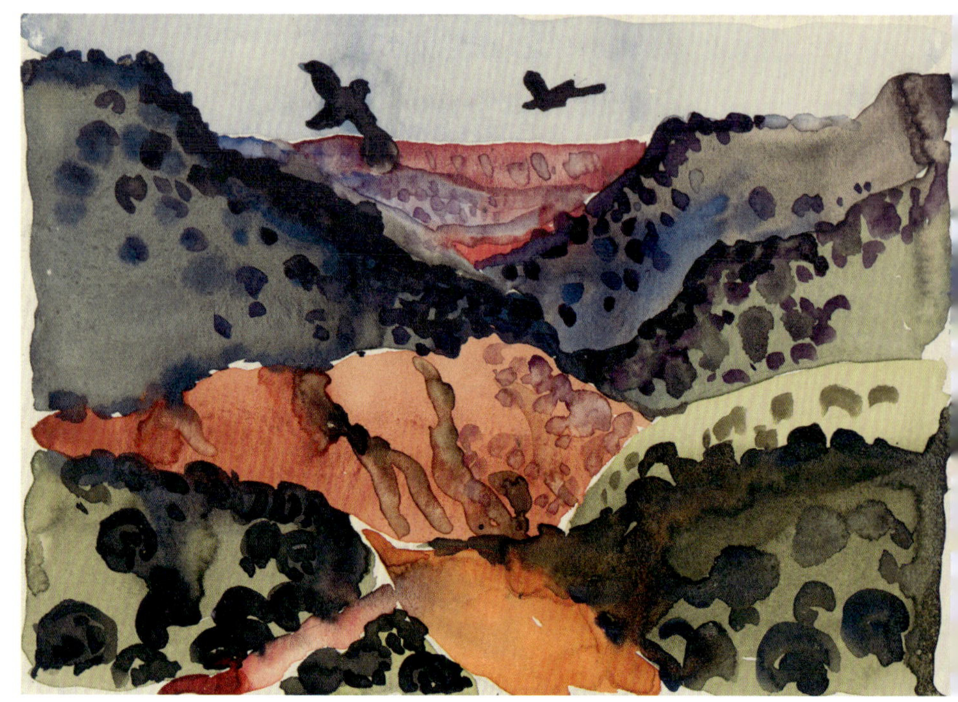

a series of watercolours titled *Evening Star I–VII* (pp.32–3). These bold abstract pictures distil the evening star O'Keeffe had seen on her walks in Canyon to broad bands of colour. She conveys with a few brushstrokes the quixotic luminosity of the star and a sense of wavelike movement that spreads convincingly across the paper. The subtle blend of transparency and opacity she employed through the medium made it an effective tool to evoke the seemingly invisible forces that lie within nature. In August 1917 she took a trip with her sister, Claudia, to Colorado and passed through New Mexico for the first time. Relaying her observations to Stieglitz in a letter, O'Keeffe marvelled at the 'space between the ground and sky ... it is tremendous – I want to stay – I've wanted to stop most every station.'[13]

NEW YORK & LAKE GEORGE

Encouraged by Strand, at Stieglitz's behest, O'Keeffe travelled back to New York on 10 June 1918. By then both of O'Keeffe's parents had passed away. The move brought her closer to Stieglitz (he had promised to financially support her for a year) and she became immediately embroiled in his New York circle, brushing shoulders with important American figures including

John Marin, Arthur Dove, Max Weber, Marsden Hartley and Charles Demuth. This artistic network was characterised by an exchange of ideas and a commitment to an American modernist art, deftly managed by Stieglitz.

As O'Keeffe and Stieglitz spent increasingly longer periods of time together, their all-consuming creative connection transformed into a deep romantic love. Although still married and twenty-three years her senior, Stieglitz began an affair with the artist. Having already staged O'Keeffe's first solo show at 291 in April 1917, he continued to promote and champion her work, encouraging her experimentation with form and colour. They collaborated on projects, cementing their profound relationship into tangible works of art, and giving each other a revitalised energy. In 1918, the fifty-four-year-old Stieglitz began a photographic series of O'Keeffe that he sustained for the next two decades. Among these portraits were a series of nudes and close-up shots of her body, focusing mostly on her hands, feet and torso. Stieglitz exhibited forty-five of these photographs, alongside other works, at the Anderson Galleries in 1921, to critical acclaim. This display added to the sexualised readings of her work fostered by critics since her first show at 291 in 1916, which the artist unequivocally refuted. Up until his death in 1946, Stieglitz produced over three hundred portraits of O'Keeffe.

Between 1918 and 1929, O'Keeffe regularly visited the Stieglitz family home near Lake George, a vast leafy resort at the southeastern base of the Adirondack Mountains, with a direct route to New York. In a letter to the writer Sherwood Anderson in 1923, O'Keeffe noted there was 'something so perfect about the mountains, and the lake and the trees'.[14] This appreciation of her surroundings governed much of O'Keeffe's artistic output in the early 1920s as she divided her time between New York and Lake George, with the occasional sojourn to Maine, Boston or Washington. Mostly painting in oils, she conveyed the stillness of the reflection in the lake's surface, as seen in *Lake George* 1922 (pp.40–1), already refining her landscapes into flattened abstracted shapes. Around the same time as she was painting the lake, she was making works which had a quality that recalled her abstractions of the previous decade. *From the Lake No. 3* (p.44) and *Red, Yellow and Black Streak* (p.45), both of which were completed in 1924, hint at the organic shapes and lines that occupied her charcoal

Canyon with Crows 1917
Watercolour and graphite on paper
2.5 × 30.5

drawings. The rhythmic curving forms sweep across the canvas, colours bleed into one another, and the landscape appears smooth yet palpable.

As early as 1922, common motifs appeared in the work of O'Keeffe and Stieglitz. One such commonality was the subject of sky and clouds. Stieglitz embarked on a series of atmospheric photographs of clouds titled *Equivalents*. O'Keeffe began to paint more representationally, pulling directly from the natural world around Lake George with paintings like *A Celebration* 1924 (opposite). Each artist dug into the essence of their subject, extolling the freedom of the sky. O'Keeffe would return to this theme in a later series of oil paintings, *Sky Above Clouds*, in the 1960s and 1970s (pp.90–1). During this time, Stieglitz and Emmeline Obermeyer divorced – and, in December 1924, O'Keeffe and Stieglitz married. As was typical of the artist, she kept her last name, and with it the artistic identity she had worked hard to cultivate.

From 1925, when in New York, she spent time on a series of oil paintings that focused on the transformed city skyline. A magnetic feeling of modernity permeated the city in the first decades of the twentieth century. The Singer Building was opened in 1908, followed by the Woolworth Building in 1913 becoming the tallest skyscraper in the world for over a decade. O'Keeffe's series of skyscrapers and panoramic views reflect this dramatic shift towards modernity, often in the style of art deco (pp.46–9).[15] *Radiator Building—Night, New York* 1927 (p.47) encapsulates the energetic and rhythmic feel of the city at night. Dominating the centre of the painting stands the American Radiator Building located on West 40th Street, an art-deco-inspired structure built in 1924. The city was an important source of inspiration for American photographers, and O'Keeffe was likely influenced by the work of Edward Steichen, Alvin Langdon Coburn, and most notably Stieglitz, who made depictions of the city at night.

Although initially taken with Lake George and the dynamism of New York, O'Keeffe grew tired of the lack of privacy and began to recognise her need for solitude and a place to work that was neither location. In the late 1920s, her relationship with Stieglitz began to show signs of breaking down as he pursued an affair with the young activist Dorothy Norman, and O'Keeffe's physical and mental health gradually deteriorated.

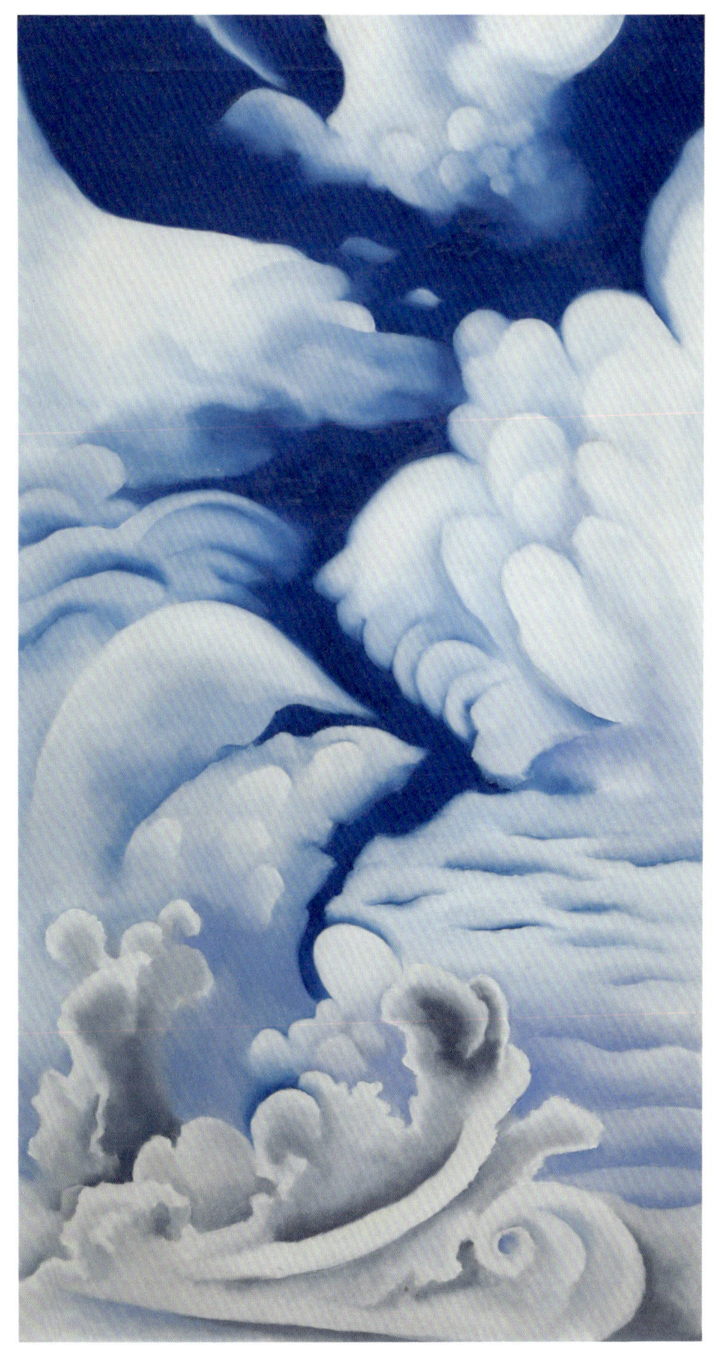

A Celebration 1924
Oil paint on canvas
88.6 × 45.7

FLOWERS

Many people will know O'Keeffe through her sumptuous paintings of flowers. O'Keeffe started painting floral subjects when studying at the Art Institute of Chicago. It was not until 1918, however, that she began to develop and hone this subject matter. *Blue Flower* 1918, one of her earliest magnified flower works, has an unusual vantage point and, when combined with the sensuous curves of the flower, connects to the broader patterns and rhythms that pervade her still lifes (p.39) and Southwest landscapes.

Most of her flower paintings were completed during the 1920s and 1930s and represent a foundation of her artistic legacy offering a unique lens through which to understand her body of work. Far from mere botanical studies, O'Keeffe's flowers are expansive and symbolic, embodying her fascination with form, colour and the relationship between nature and 'inner harmony'. Indeed, works such as *Dark Iris No. III* 1927 (p.51) transform the delicate structures of the iris petals into abstract ethereal worlds. Native to southern China, the flower blooms for short periods during the year. Symbolic of mystery and elegance, O'Keeffe's irises invite the viewer to experience nature on a seemingly transcendental level.

At the time, these paintings were not merely aesthetic triumphs but were considered by some as tied to O'Keeffe's sex. Critics interpreted the undulating forms and luminosity of O'Keeffe's flowers as expressions of feminine power and sexuality. However, as art historian Griselda Pollock has stated, O'Keeffe's flower works have 'mistakenly come to stand for the displaced sex and body'.[16] Moreover, O'Keeffe herself resisted such interpretations, suggesting her flowers were a way of seeing replete with joy and reverie for the natural world.

As with most of her flower paintings, the entirety of the picture plane was important for O'Keeffe. In both *Oriental Poppies* 1927 (pp.52–3) and *Two Calla Lilies on Pink* 1928 (opposite), O'Keeffe elected to fill the frame with two identical flowers. Viewing paintings like *Two Calla Lilies on Pink*, we see again the strong connection O'Keeffe had with her artistic peers. One such contemporary was the photographer Imogen Cunningham, a member of the renowned f/64 group along with O'Keeffe's close friend, the photographer Ansel Adams. Cunningham's photograph *Two Callas* ?1925–9 did what Strand's earlier *Abstraction, Bowls* 1916 accomplished: close-range shots of everyday subject matter elevated to fine art.

Two Calla Lilies on Pink
1928
Oil paint on canvas
101.6 × 76.2

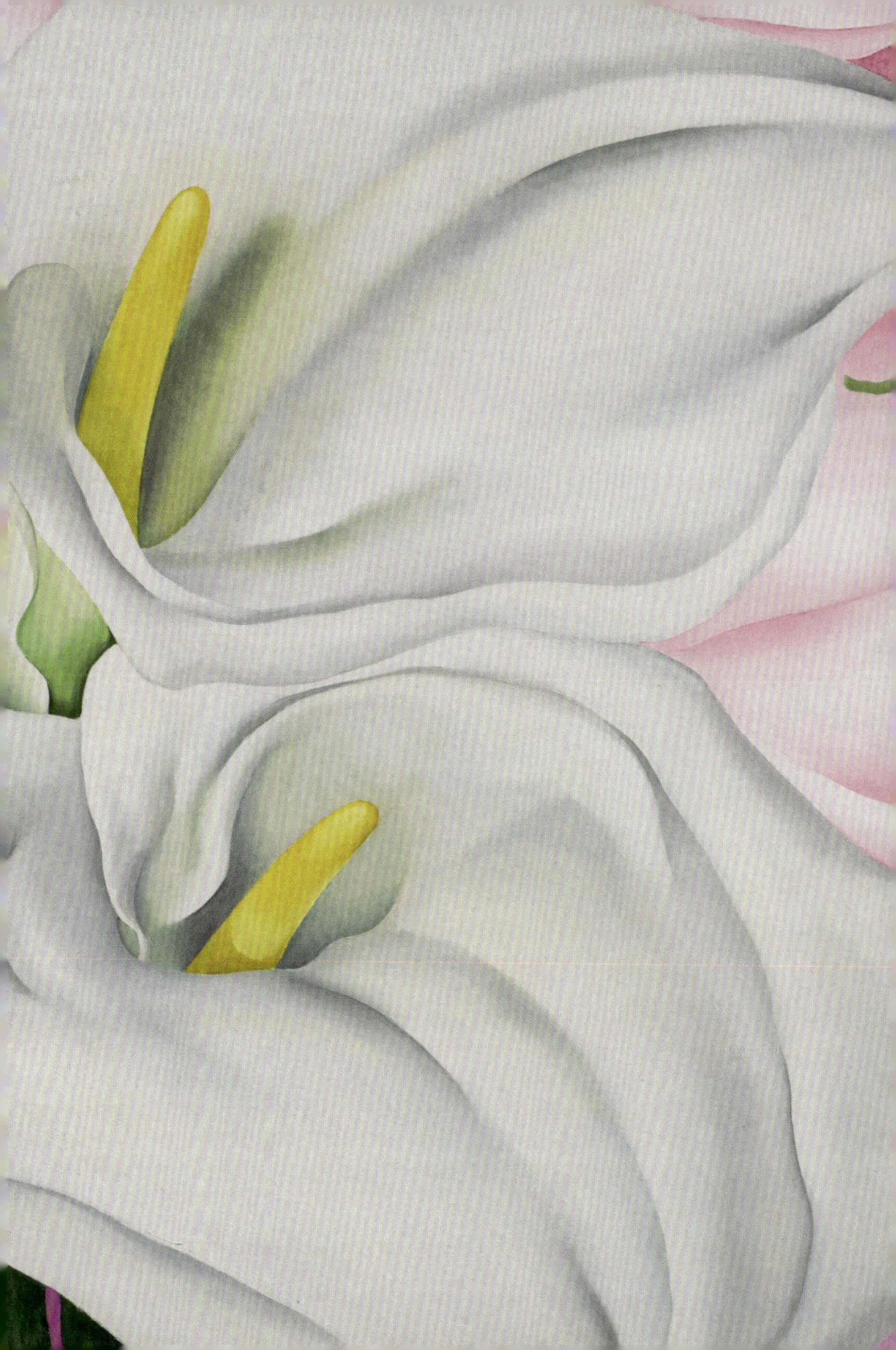

DIVIDED SELF: NEW MEXICO

I am divided between my man and a life with him – and something of the outdoors – of your world – that is in my blood – and that I know I will never get rid of – I have to get along with my divided self the best way I can.[17]

O'Keeffe's first, brief visit to New Mexico in August 1917, rich with the spirit of the sky and land, had a lasting effect on her. Nevertheless, she did not return until the summer of 1929. With her close friend Beck (Rebecca) Strand – who was married to Paul Strand – she visited Mabel Luhan Dodge, a socialite and progressive patron of the arts, who encouraged O'Keeffe to spend her summer in Taos. The Strands had visited Dodge and her Pueblo Indian husband Tony Luhan before (the couple's ranch was a creative hub for artists, writers and photographers) and conveyed the beauty and splendour to O'Keeffe. Here, she worked from a studio provided by Dodge. Writing to Stieglitz in May 1929, she marvelled at the 'unimaginable dream' she was experiencing.[18]

Ranchos Church 1930 (opposite) was made during this early trip. In the painting, the church – an eighteenth-century colonial structure – seemingly protrudes from the ground. The grey and white clouds fan out from behind the sand-coloured adobe building, producing a somewhat mystical composition. Despite the sharp definition of the structure's outline, it appears to connect earth and sky, perhaps signifying a connection between the human and spiritual realm – an idea that O'Keeffe would later explore in her depictions of pelvic bones set against the clear blue sky (pp.68–9). After returning to New York that autumn, O'Keeffe had her first exhibition at An American Place, Stieglitz's third and final gallery, in February 1930. The show featured many works she had painted while in New Mexico,[19] but it was met with mixed reviews.

O'Keeffe travelled west every summer for the next twenty years but would continue to spend time in New York and Lake George to schedule annual exhibitions and visit Stieglitz, with prolonged gaps between each visit. The freedom and solitude of the desert proved beneficial. She missed Stieglitz and felt conflicted between the new possibilities the landscape provided and the caring responsibilities towards her husband. Nonetheless, she had found a deep satisfaction in the radiance of New Mexico that reminded her of her childhood in Sun Prairie, Wisconsin, and her time living in Texas.

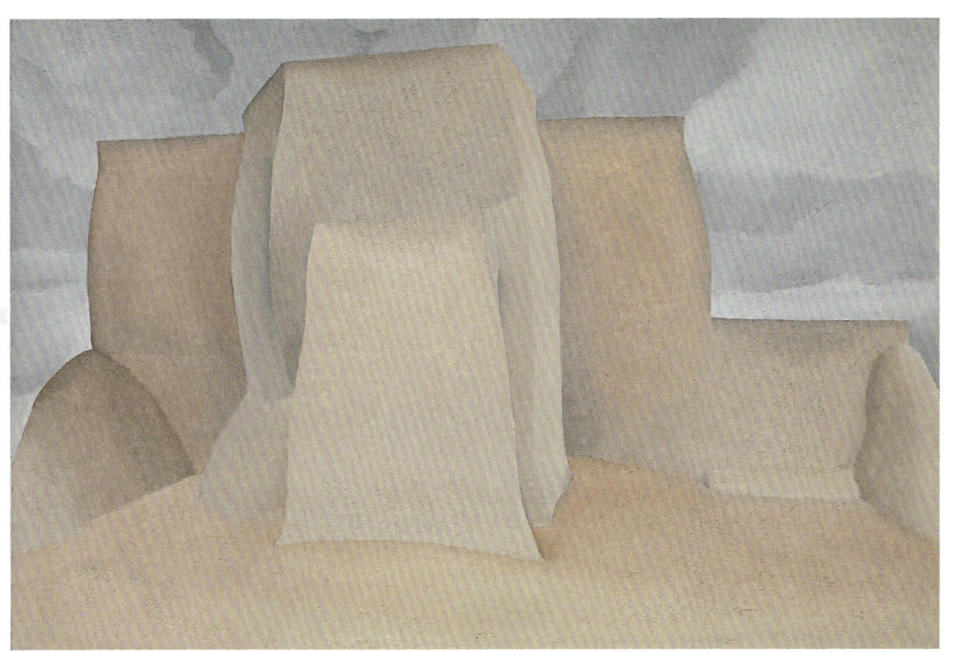

ARTIST AS COLLECTOR

Collecting objects was an important part of O'Keeffe's creative process. She was interested in the natural detritus she found on her walks along the coast in Maine, in the forests and at the waterside of Lake George, and through the desert in New Mexico. In 1926, during a trip to her friends the Schaufflers, at York Beach in Maine, O'Keeffe collected seaweed and shells that she then incorporated into still life compositions, while Stieglitz remained in Lake George. She wrote to Stieglitz: 'After breakfast I looked over all my shells that I have been picking up since I am here ... sorted out the ones I wanted ... walking – alone – I had a very good time all by myself.'[20] Her trips reflected her growing desire for solitude and an escape from the bustling city of New York and the domestic chaos of Lake George.

O'Keeffe painted animal carcasses as early as 1908, when studying at the Art Students League. From 1930s onwards, after spending the summer in New Mexico, she truly started to explore the potential of animal remnants and other found matter in her work. She began collecting bones and skulls, admiring their striking sun-bleached forms. She understood them as 'symbols of the desert', citing them as 'strangely

Ranchos Church 1930
Oil paint on canvas
61 × 91.4

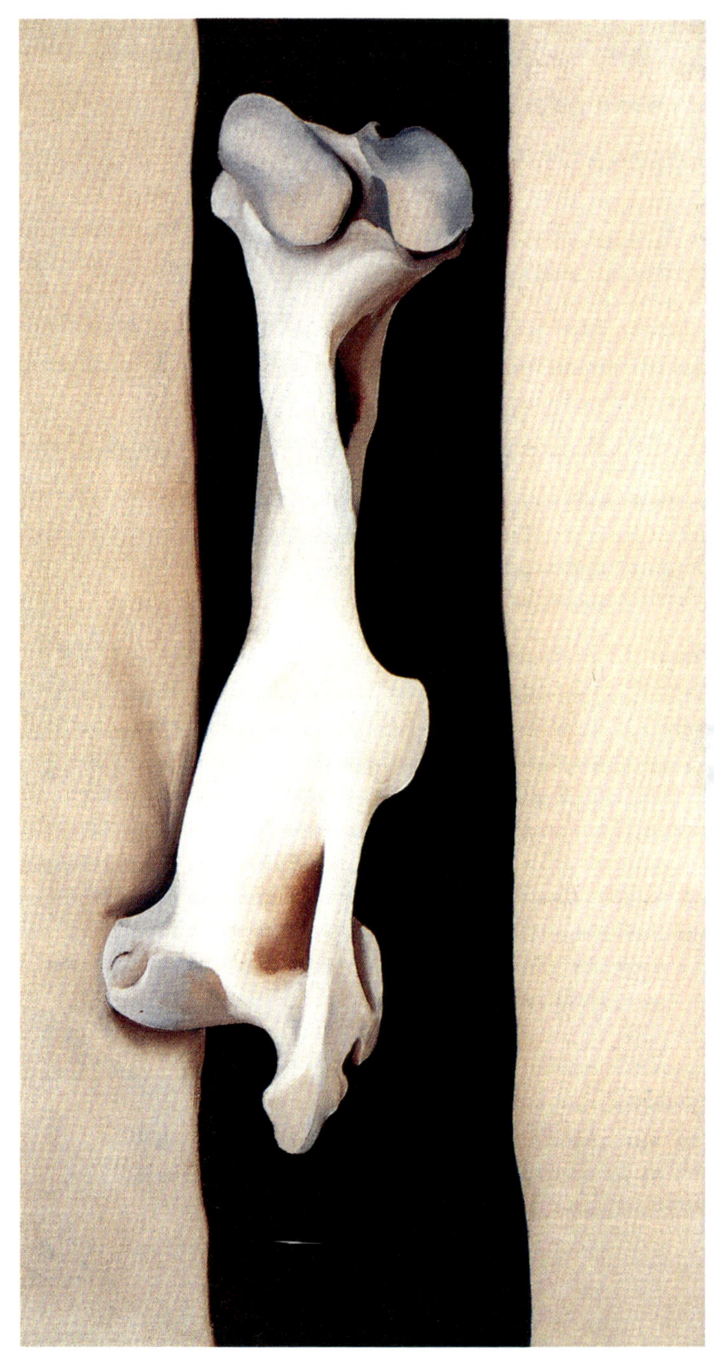

Thigh Bone on Black Stripe
1930
Oil paint on canvas
76.2 × 40

more living than the animals walking around'.[21] Like her shell paintings (p.61), her bone works draw on the familiar art-historical genre of still life and landscape painting, yet offer a uniquely complex and multilayered version of a representational painting (pp.56, 58–60). One of the more arresting early bone paintings is *Thigh Bone on Black Stripe* 1930 (opposite). Here, O'Keeffe places a singular stark white thigh bone vertically in the centre of the canvas, juxtaposed against the wide black stripe that sits behind. Precisely flanked on either side are two sand-coloured strips, the symmetry of which creates a visually compelling composition. By placing the bone on its own at the centre of the picture plane, she undergirds a sense of mystical reverie or relic-like idolatry.

O'Keeffe also collected artificial flowers while in New Mexico. She integrated them into paintings, including her emblematic *Summer Days* 1936 (p.59). Above all, O'Keeffe took delight, both physical and emotional, in the sustenance derived from collecting such objects which she then translated into monumental works of art. In later life, as her eyesight began to deteriorate, she found comfort in the tactility of her rock collection.

SPIRIT OF SOLITUDE

As soon as I saw it, that was my country.
I'd never seen anything like it before, but it fitted to me exactly.
It's something that's in the air ...
The sky is different, the stars are different, the wind is different.
I shouldn't say too much about this because other people may get interested and I don't want them interested.[22]

The increasingly high profits from artwork sales mid-century afforded O'Keeffe an economic independence crucial for her creative and personal evolution. Having visited Ghost Ranch for the first time in August 1934, she later, in 1940, purchased Ranchos de los Burros, a small adobe house close to the ranch, foregrounding her commitment to the area.

The 'Black Place' paintings (p.71), a well-known body of work created in the 1940s, came from a place of quiet resolution. Compelled by the preternatural geological formations around the Bisti Badlands, some 150 km (90 miles) west of Ghost Ranch, O'Keeffe executed twenty-six works that evoke the deep personal connection she had with the landscape. Alongside the limited series of 'White Place' paintings (p.70), also made in the 1940s, her 'Black Place' paintings are dynamic and emotionally charged. Negative space constitutes an important aspect of the 'White Place' series, like her pelvic bone works, whereas the 'Black Place' paintings fill the whole picture plane. O'Keeffe worked in all kinds of weather; her determination to paint was unceasing. An early riser, she spent entire days exploring the desert, leaving the house at dawn and returning in the evening. One of her great pleasures in life was hiking and she would often camp in the wilderness, walking and sketching, and sometimes, whilst still out in the desert, would set up her easel in the back of the car and paint.

In May 1946, the Museum of Modern Art in New York staged a major retrospective of O'Keeffe's work – the first at the museum solely dedicated to a woman. In early summer she returned to New Mexico, but her trip was cut short when the news reached her that Stieglitz had suffered a stroke on 10 July. She travelled back to New York to find Stieglitz in a coma; he died three days later. O'Keeffe spent the next two years organising, cataloguing and distributing his vast estate.

Emotionally and artistically free from the constraints of modern life, newly widowed, and always adamant to do what she wanted, in 1949 she finally settled in New Mexico. The home she built in Abiquiú was constantly changing. Her environment was crucial to her process, and she approached it holistically. Here, she had room to create a studio that catered to bigger paintings and she converted the living space into a workspace with large picture windows and an open layout, redesigning the house to match the importance she placed on her work.

It was in Abiquiú that O'Keeffe produced the significant series of 'Patio' paintings between 1946 and 1960 (pp.78–9). Like the minimalists' works of the 1960s, O'Keeffe's 'Patio' paintings – featuring the famous studio door – were precise and controlled, reflecting the self-assurance and discipline she embodied. In the formalist tradition, she reduced the patio tiles and door to neatly divided rectangles and squares, placing onus on the horizontality and openness of the picture.

In a similar vein, *Winter Road I* 1963 (opposite), conveys this sense of control. O'Keeffe drew the singular bulging line that curves around the edge of the canvas with a confidence demonstrating her instinctive tendency towards simplicity. From a window of the hilltop house in Abiquiú, she

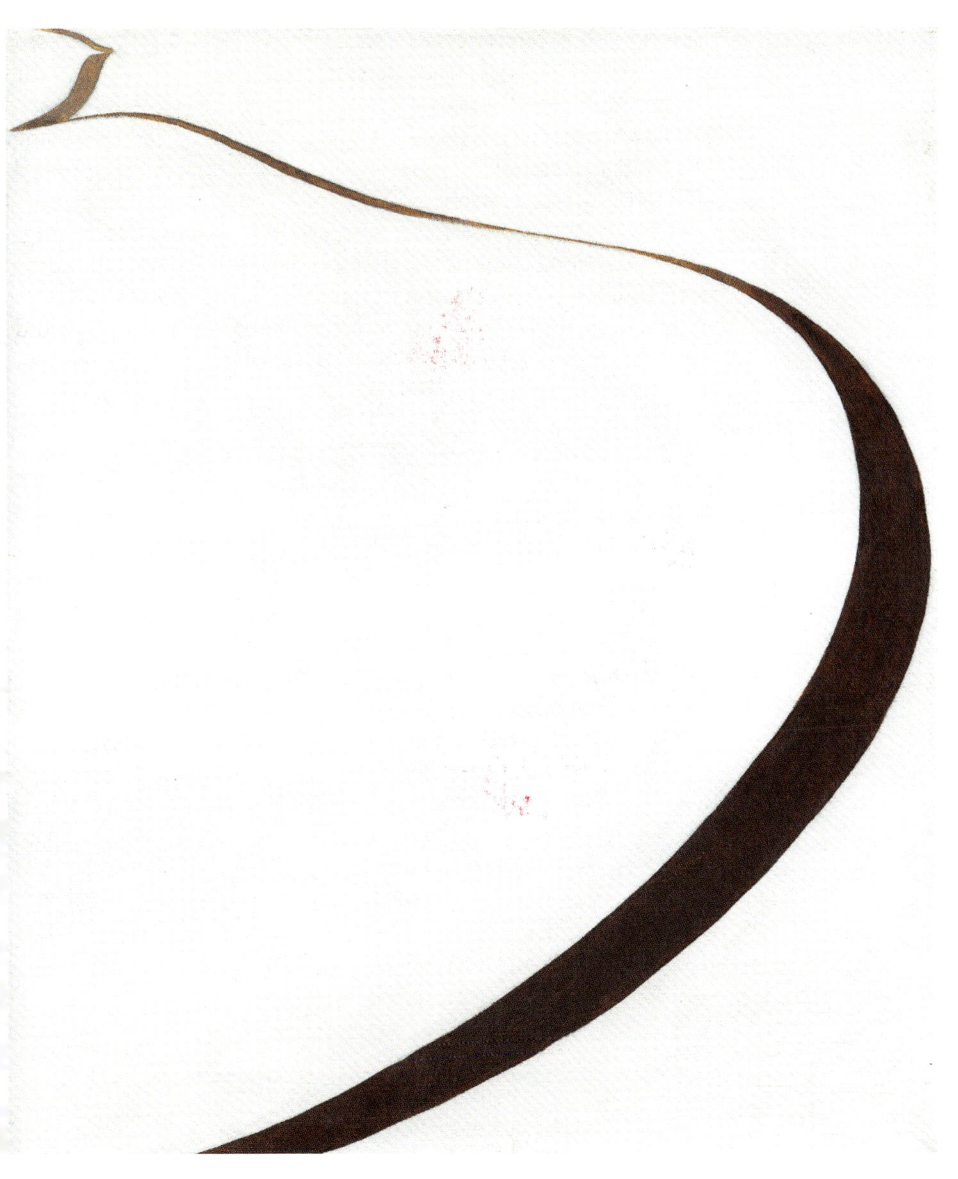

Winter Road I 1963
Oil paint on canvas
55.9 × 45.7

photographed the isolated road that seemed to 'wind away far up and down'.[23] Painting from the photograph, and perhaps partly from memory, she captures the spirit of the scene.

Between the 1950s and 1970s, O'Keeffe travelled frequently, visiting Peru, Mexico, Hawaii, Japan, the Philippines, Hong Kong, India, the Middle East and many countries in Europe, among other destinations. The work she produced during this peripatetic period distilled what she saw from the air – flying in newly established jet planes above the clouds and meandering rivers – into her largest works to date, including *Sky Above Clouds IV* 1965 (pp.90–1), standing at over two metres high and seven metres wide.

LIMINAL SPACE: THE LAST DECADES

O'Keeffe never remarried. She committed to a life far away from people but near to the things she held dear: the ability to travel, the stillness and sense of peace she felt within the desert, and a disciplined creativity. Although solitude was sacred to O'Keeffe, she was no recluse. The numerous letters she sent and received testify to the many relationships she nurtured, both personal and professional. She would also on occasion welcome to her home artists, photographers, writers, friends and family who made the pilgrimage to Ghost Ranch, although she was irritated by, and often turned away, uninvited visitors.

A turning point came in 1970 when a major touring retrospective opened at the Whitney Museum of American Art.[24] The show saw O'Keeffe achieve a newfound recognition and appreciation from younger generations. Moreover, her work had entered notable American collections by this time, including the Smithsonian American Art Museum, Museum of Modern Art, the Metropolitan Museum of Art and the Art Institute of Chicago.

By 1972, O'Keeffe's macular degeneration – a common condition that hinders a person's central vision – prevented her from painting. The following year she met twenty-seven-year-old ceramicist Juan Hamilton. O'Keeffe still possessed a sharp wit and a formidable character, and the pair struck up an unconventional companionship. With her deteriorating eyesight and unable to paint, she grew ever more reliant on Hamilton; they travelled, worked and, in her final years, lived together.

In 1977, Hamilton took over from Doris Bry as O'Keeffe's

agent.[25] Due to a rapid decline in her health, in 1984 she moved to Santa Fe, unable to remain in the remote desert far from medical facilities. O'Keeffe died on 6 March 1986 just over a year shy of her hundredth birthday. Hamilton followed her wishes and scattered her ashes at the base of the Cerro Pedernal, the mesa she had called her back yard.

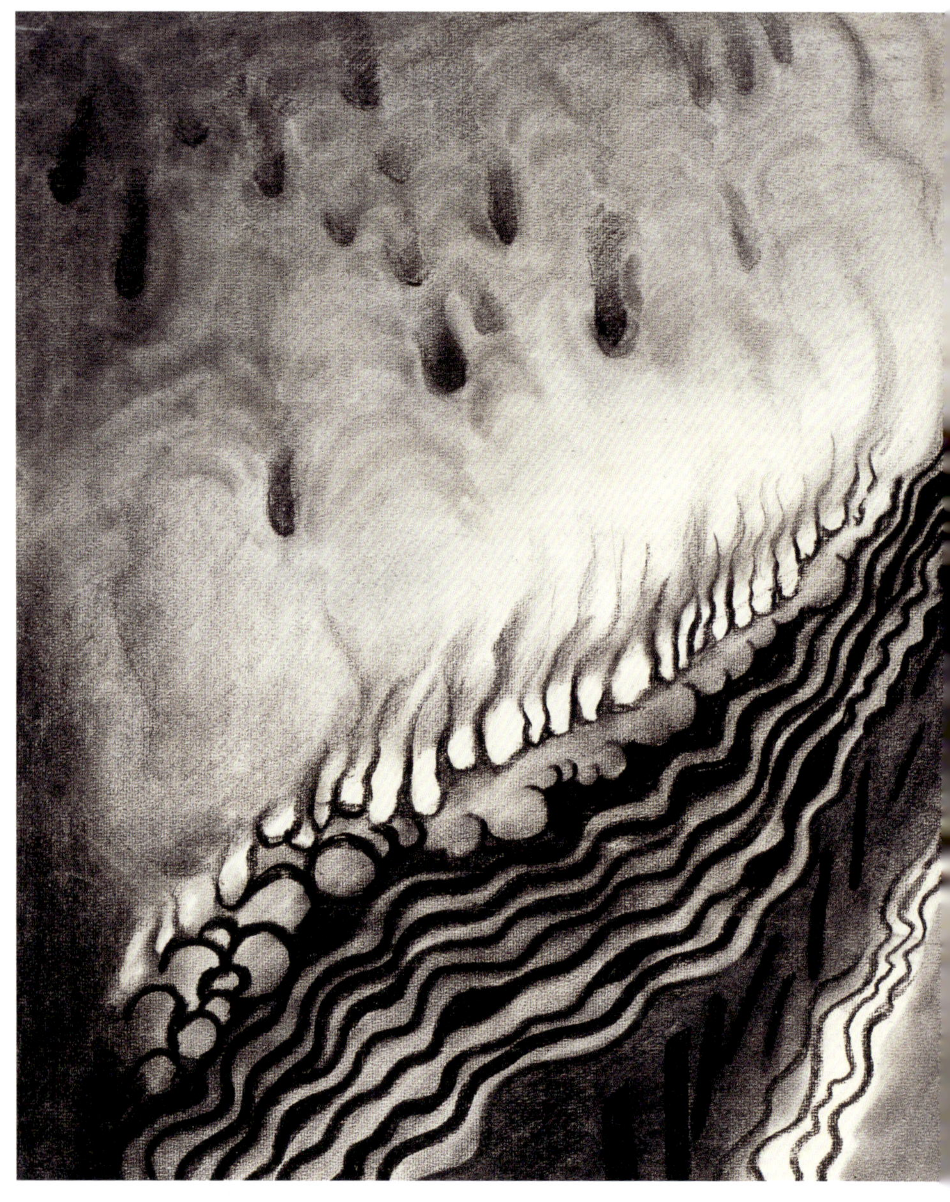

Special No.9 1915
Charcoal on paper
63.5 × 48.6

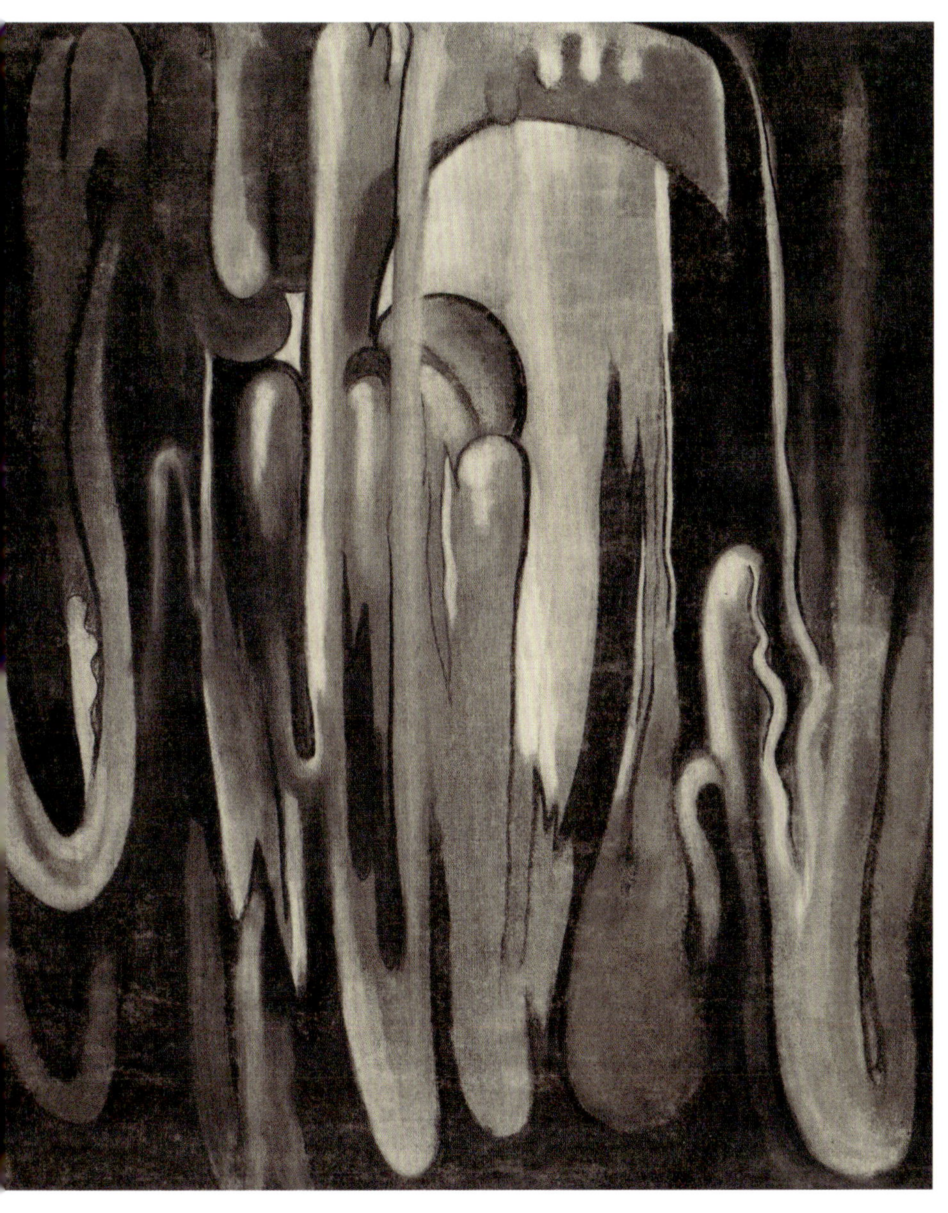

No.5 *Special* 1915
Charcoal on paper
61 × 47

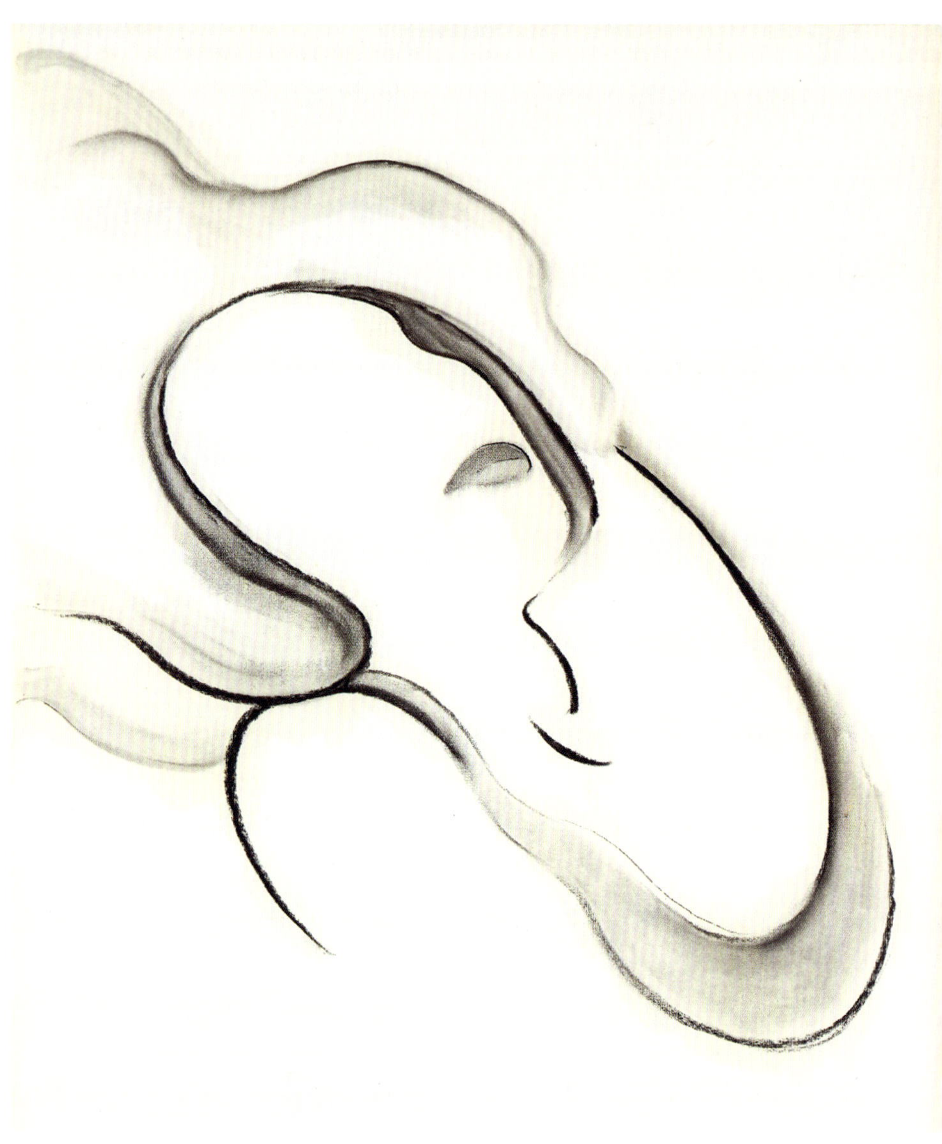

Abstraction IX 1916
Charcoal and wash on paper
63.2 × 48.3

Black Lines 1916
Watercolour on paper
62.2 × 47

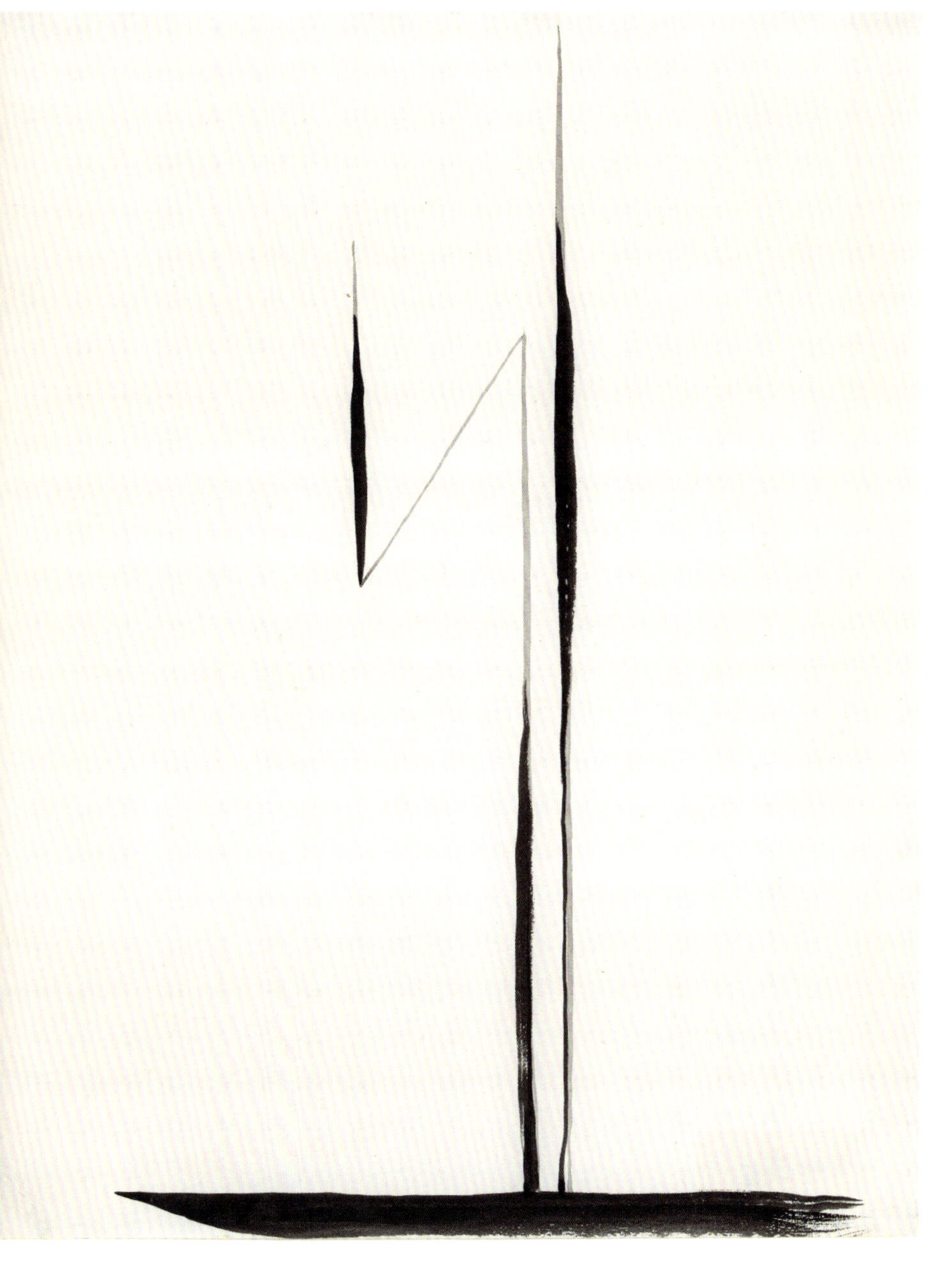

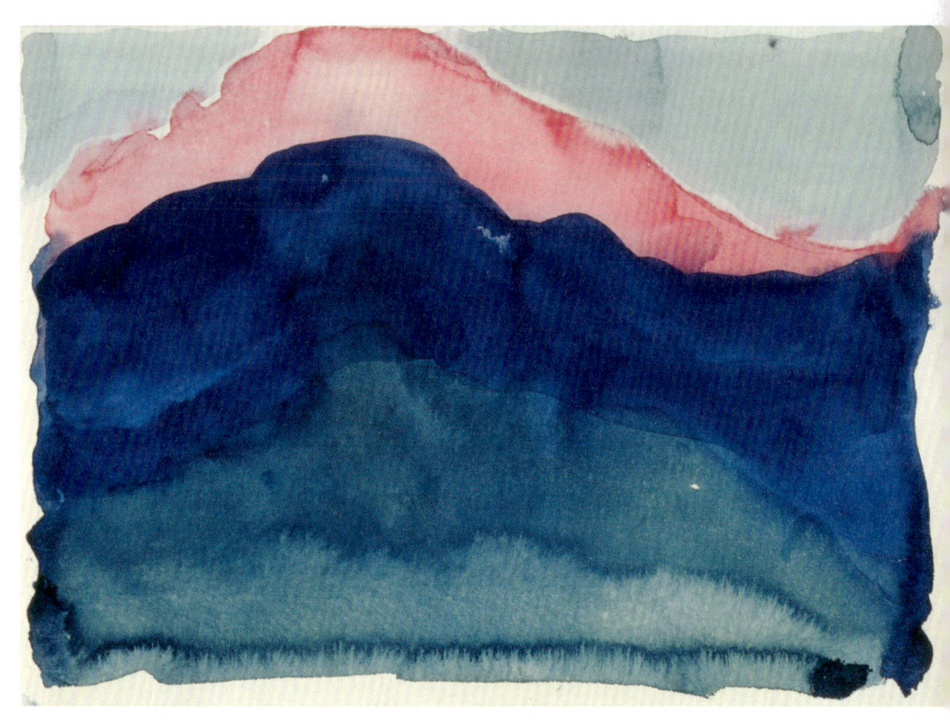

Pink and Blue Mountain 1916
Watercolour on paper
22.3 × 30.2

Blue I 1916
Watercolour on paper
78.3 × 56.5

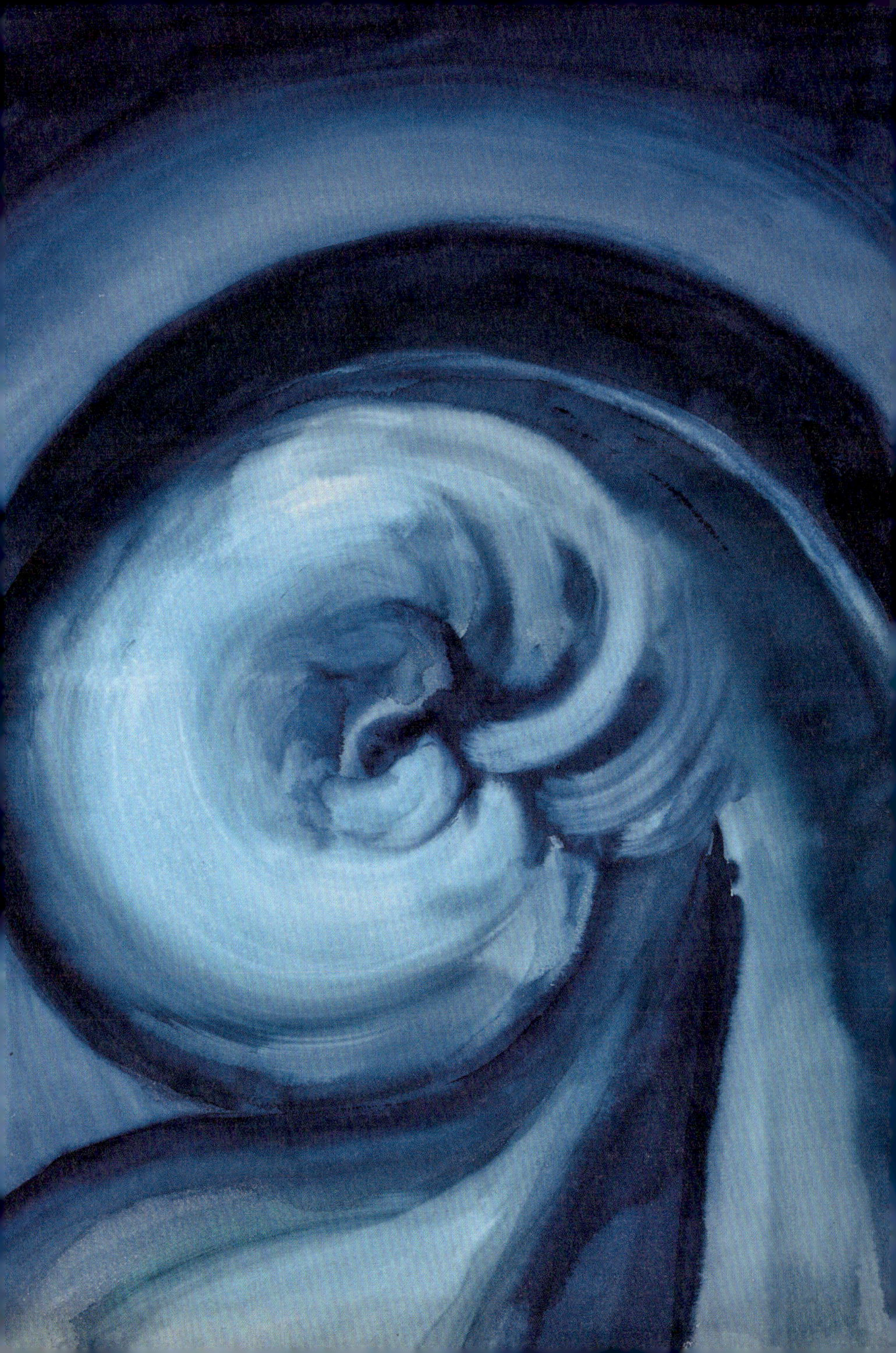

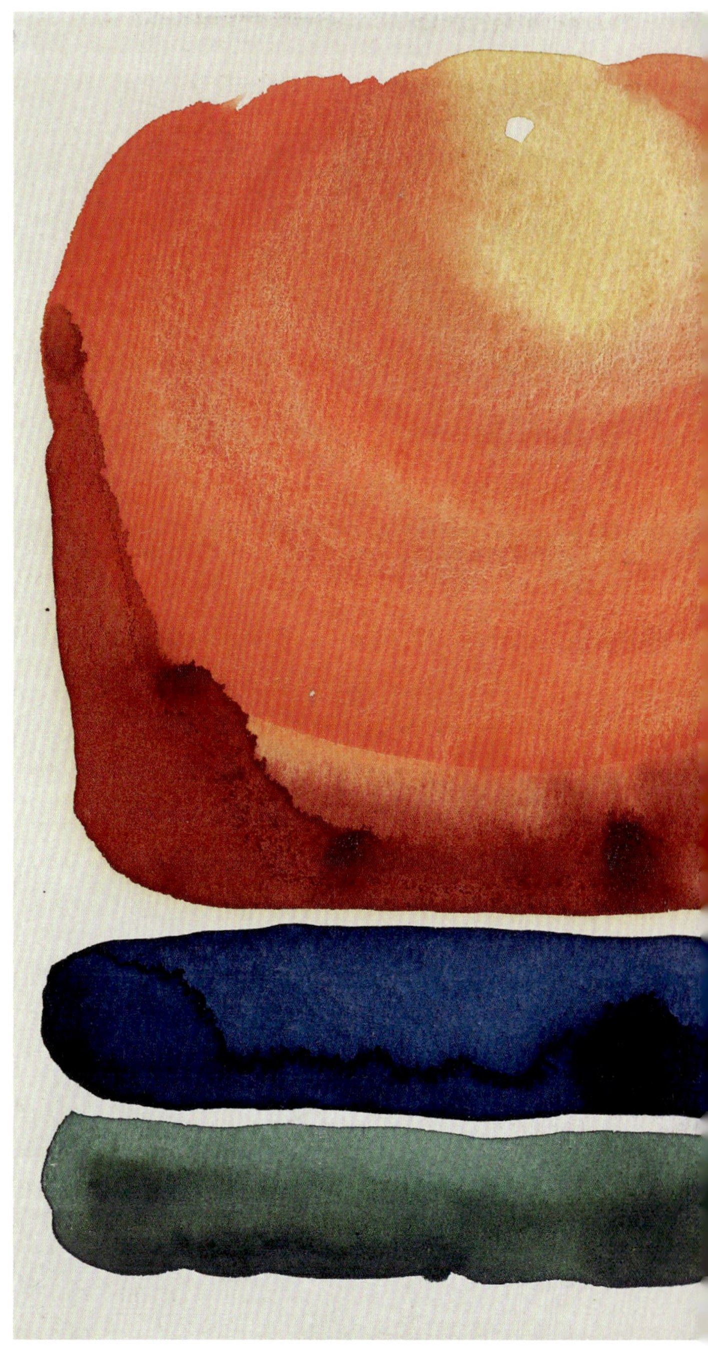

Evening Star No.II 1917
Watercolour on paper
22.2 × 30.5

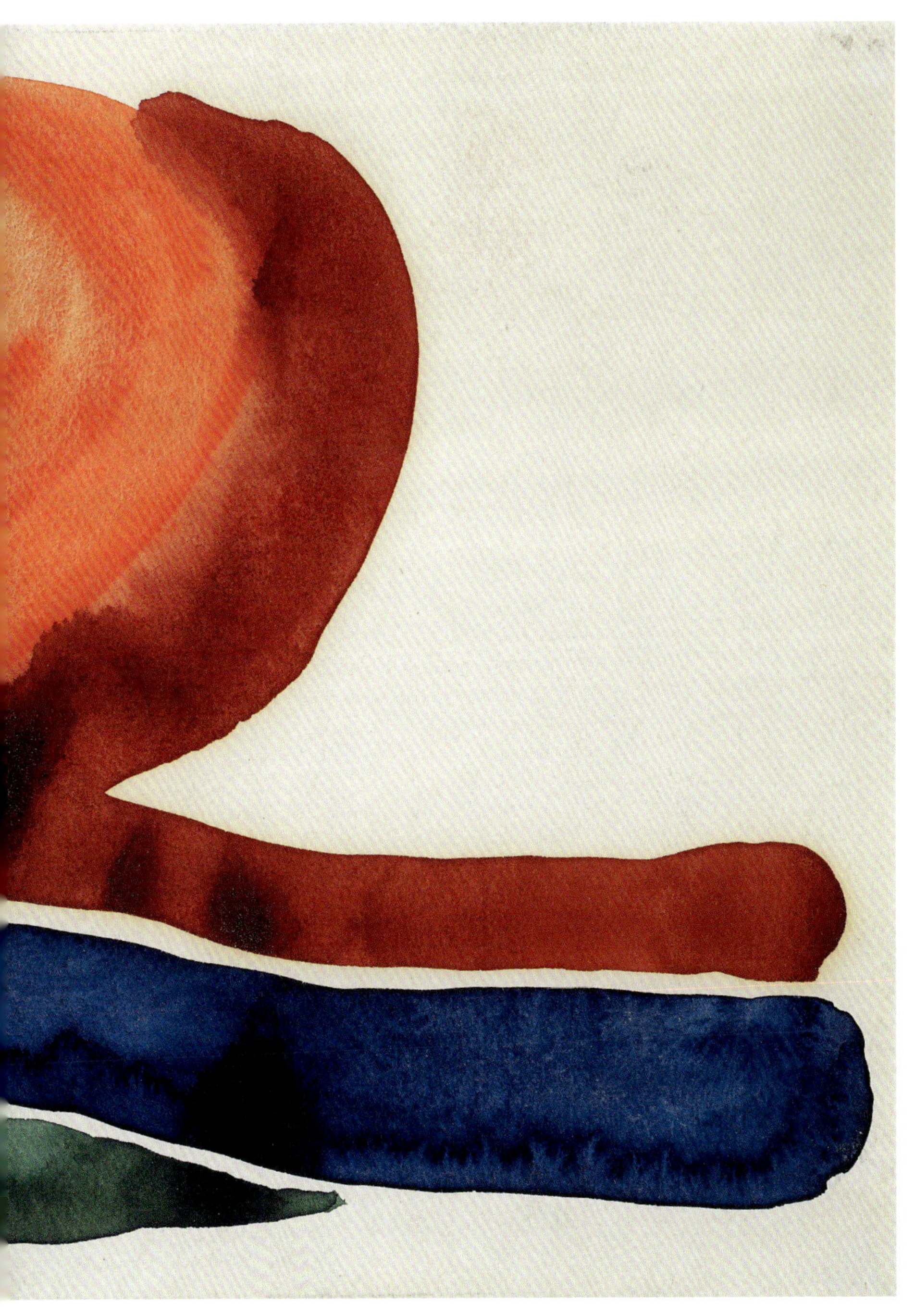

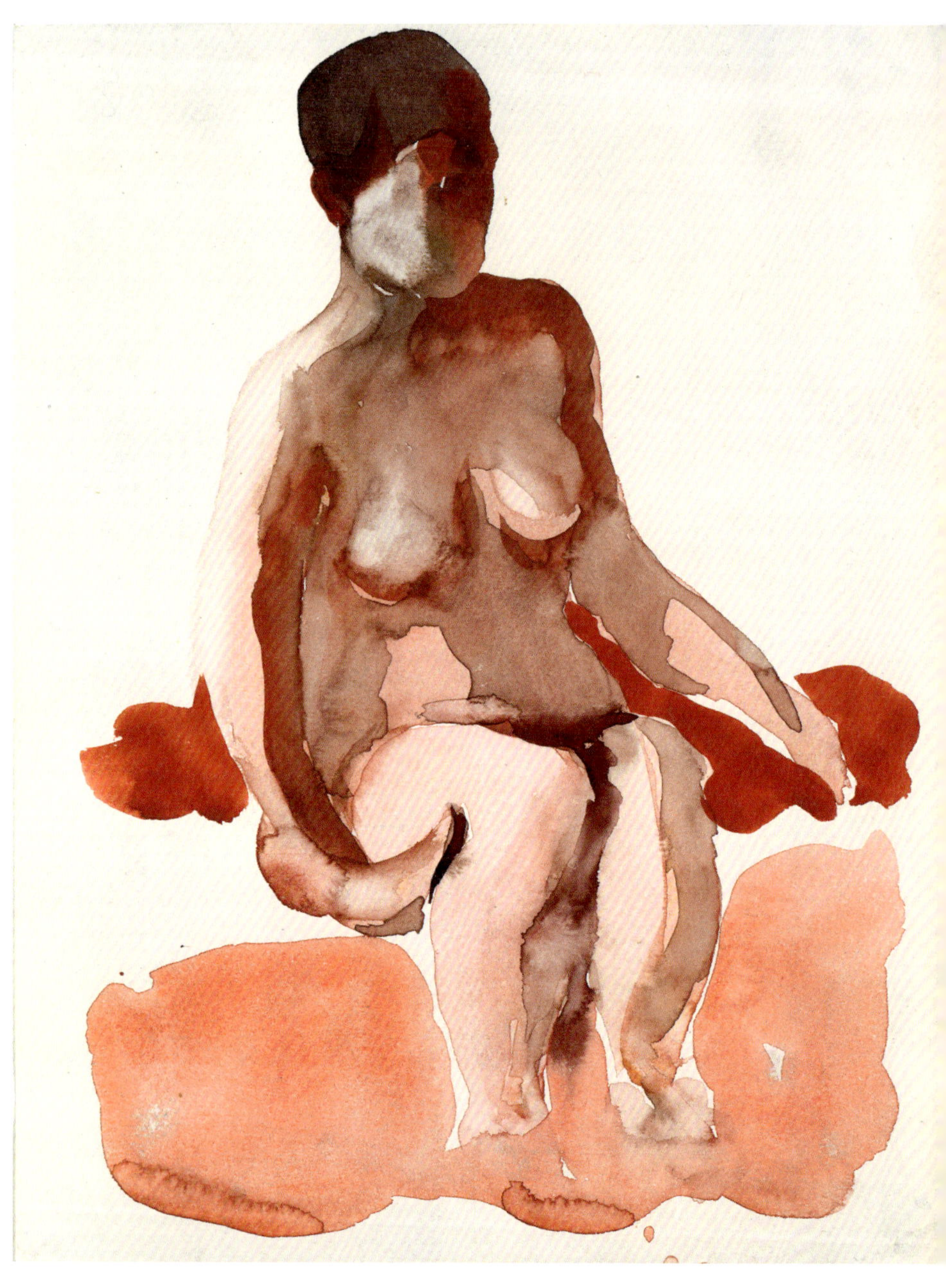

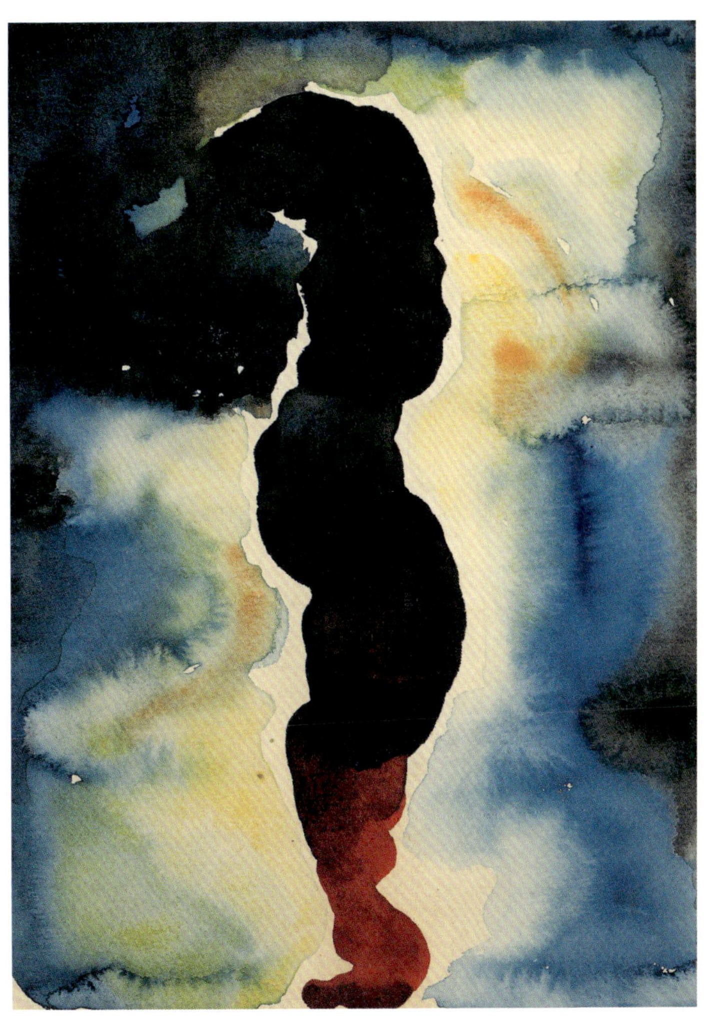

Seated Nude X 1917
Watercolour on paper
30.4 × 22.7

Untitled (Abstraction Portrait of Paul Strand) 1917
Watercolour on paper
30.5 × 22.6

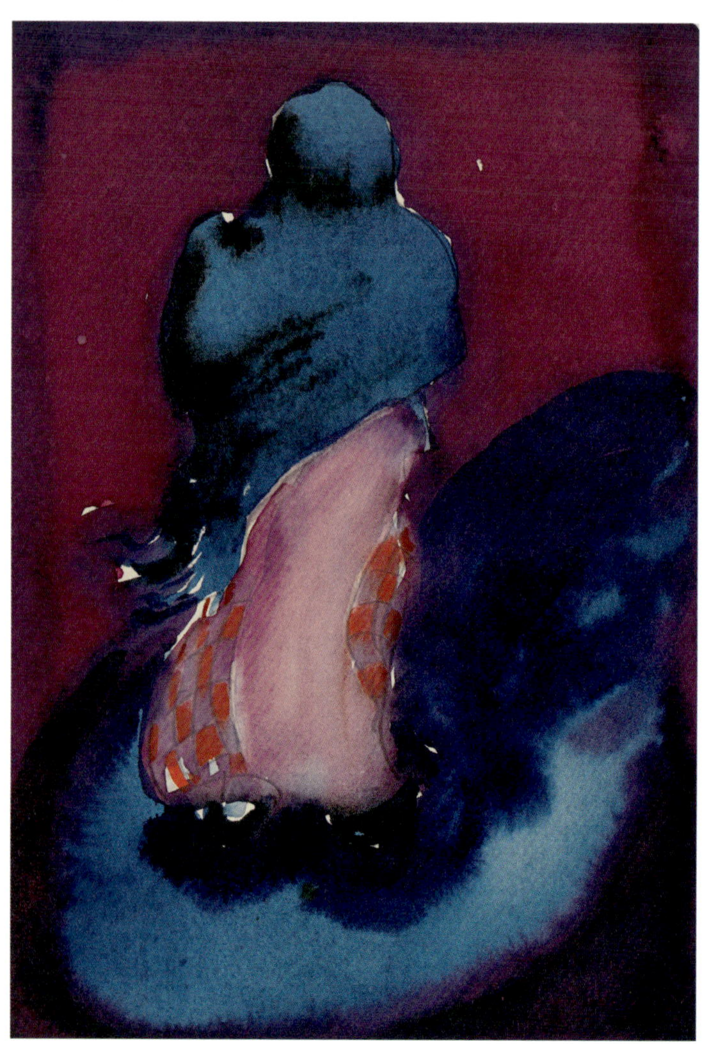

Woman with Blue Shawl 1918
Watercolour, graphite
and charcoal on paper
22.5 × 15.2

Series 1 – No.1 1918
Oil paint on composition
board
50.2 × 40.6

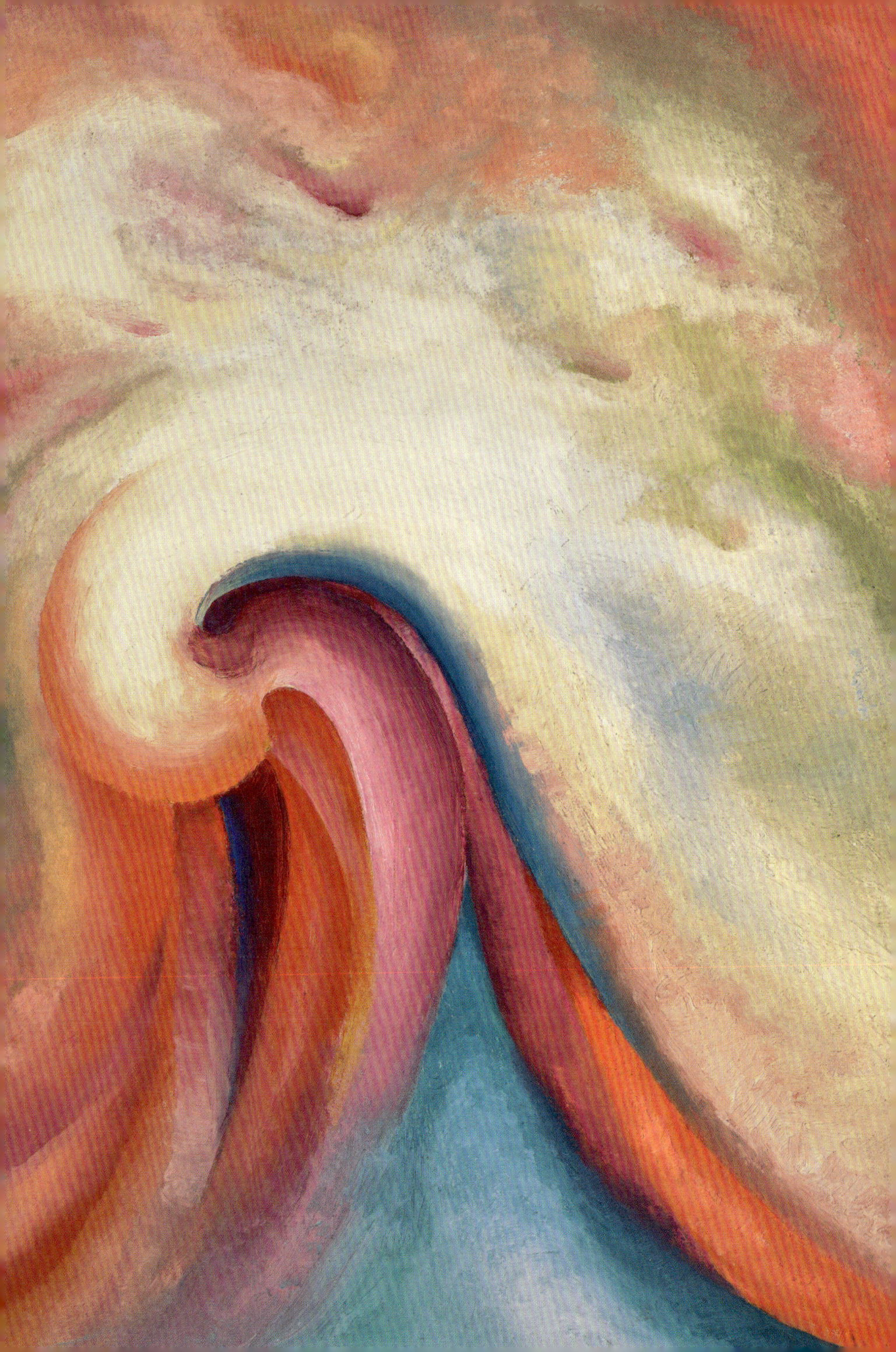

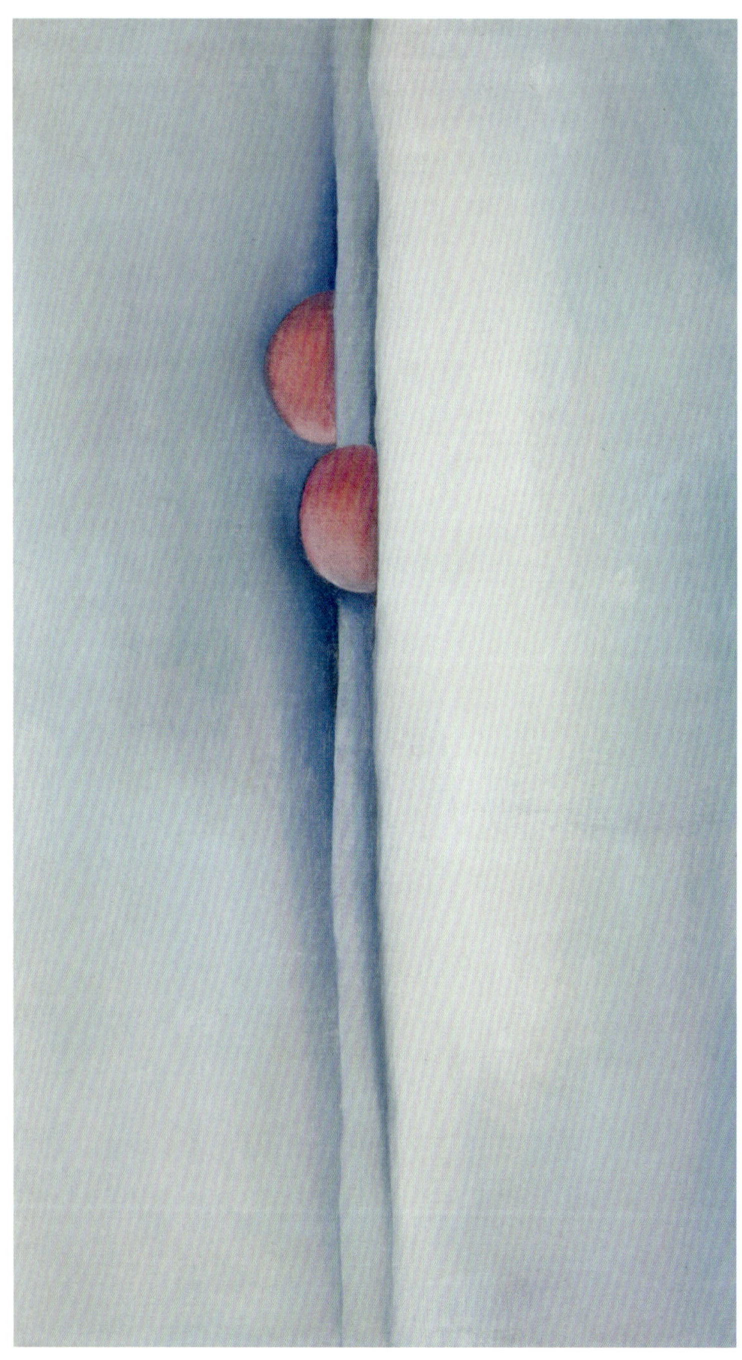

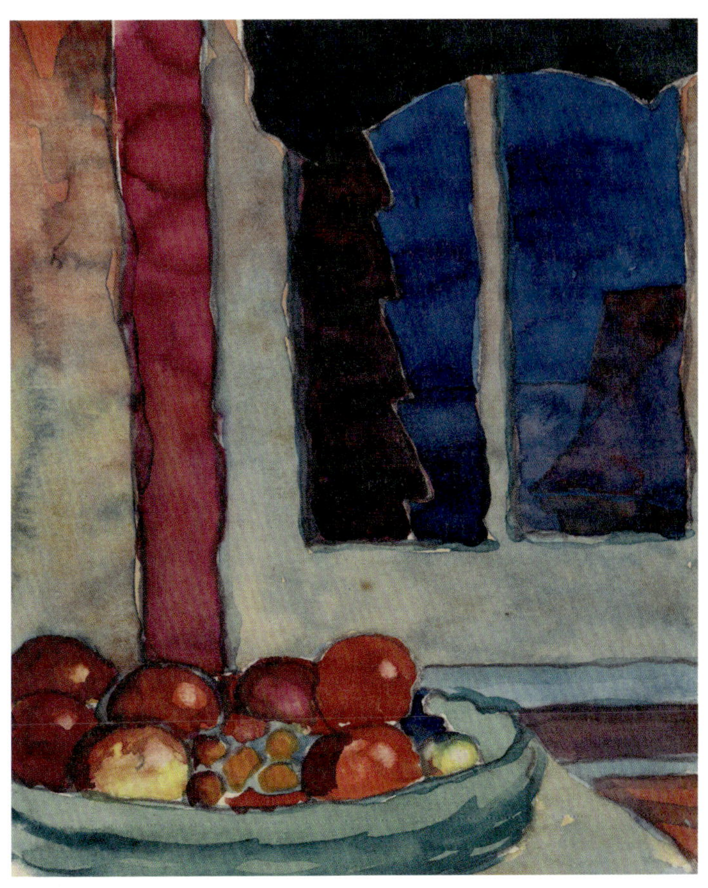

Green Lines and Pink 1919
Oil paint on canvas
45.7 × 25.4

Untitled (Bowl of Fruit) 1918
Watercolour and graphite on paper
11.5 × 76.2

OVERLEAF
Lake George [formerly *Reflection Seascape*] 1922
Oil paint on canvas
41.3 × 55.9

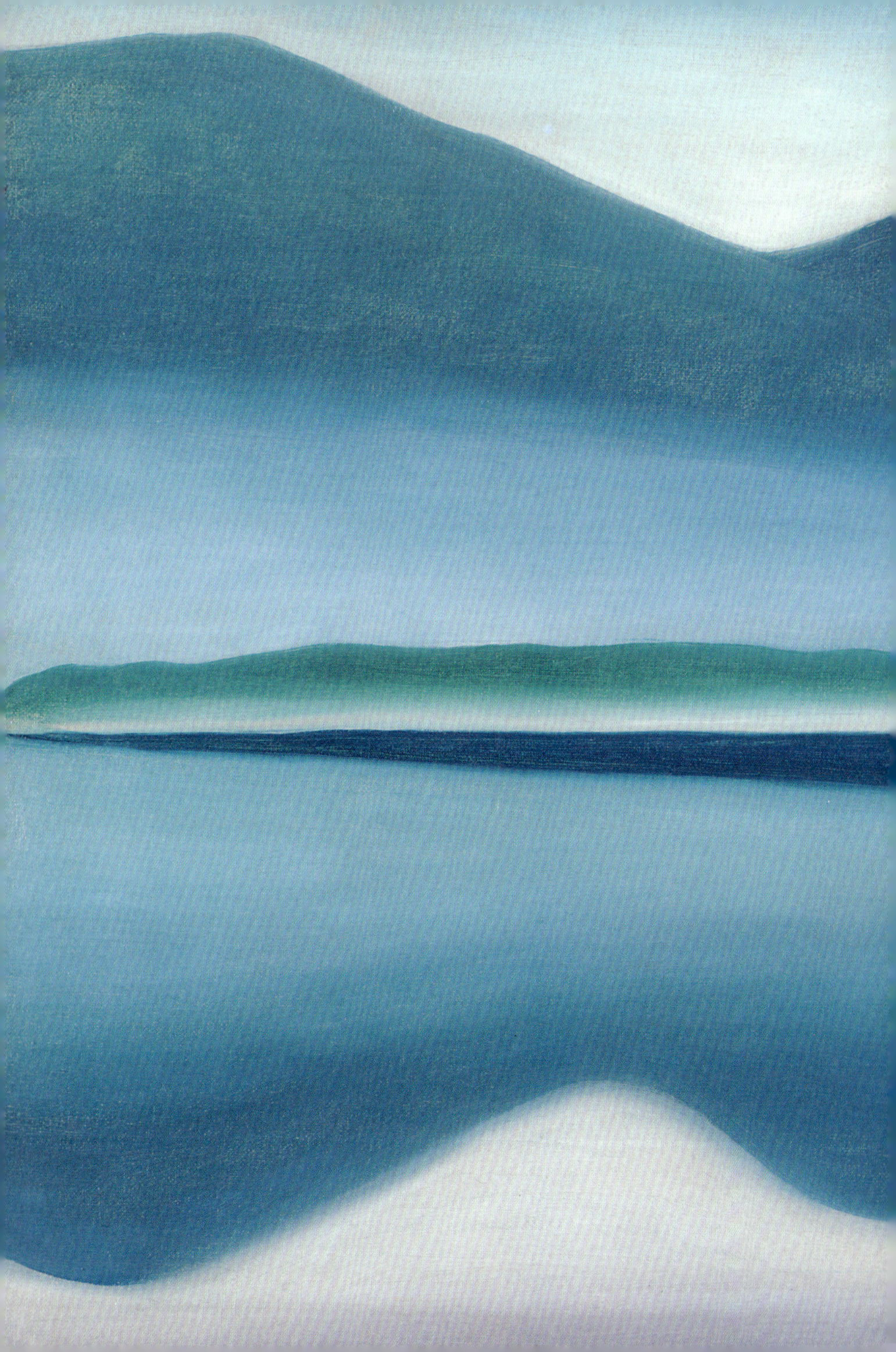

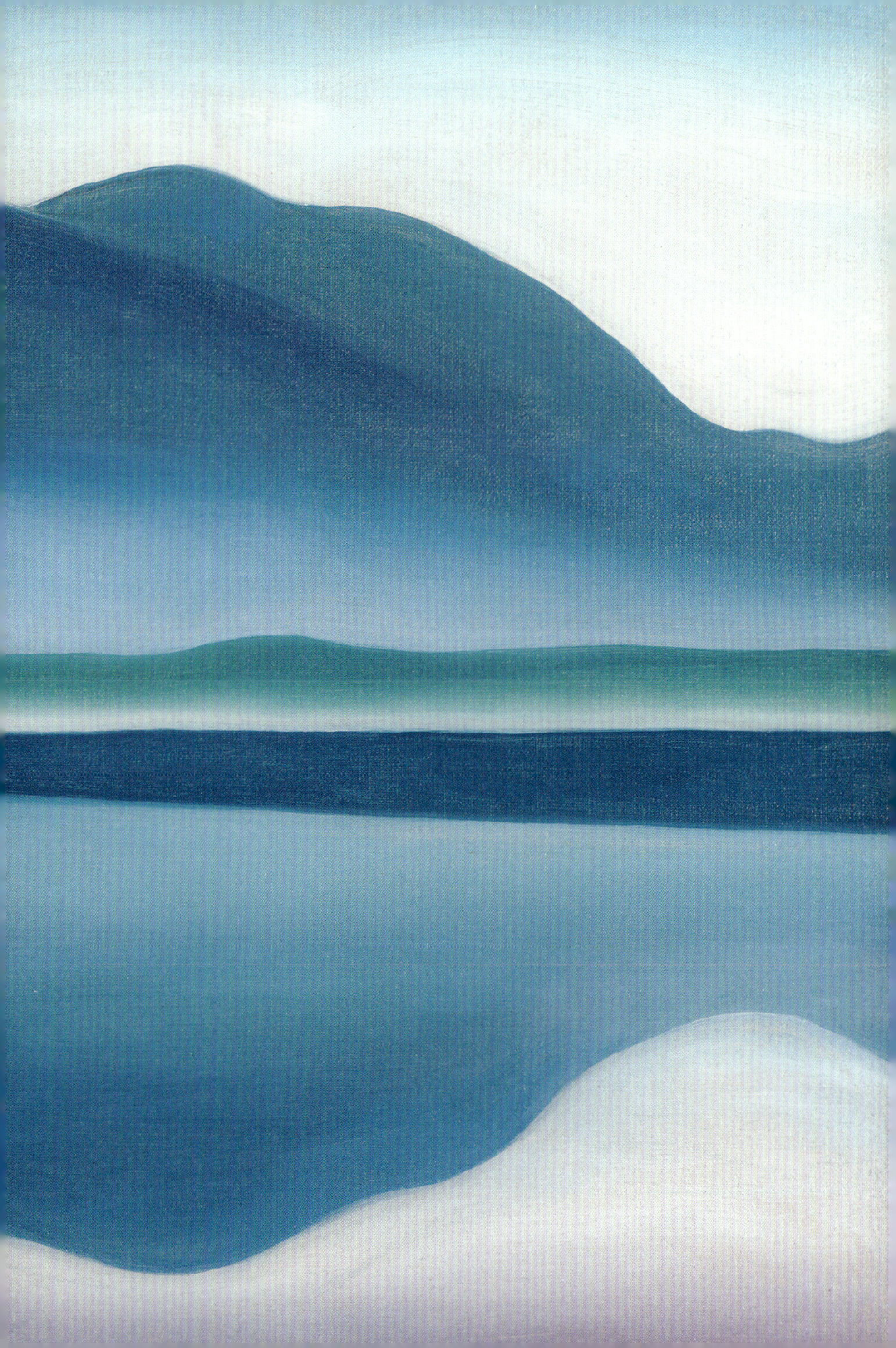

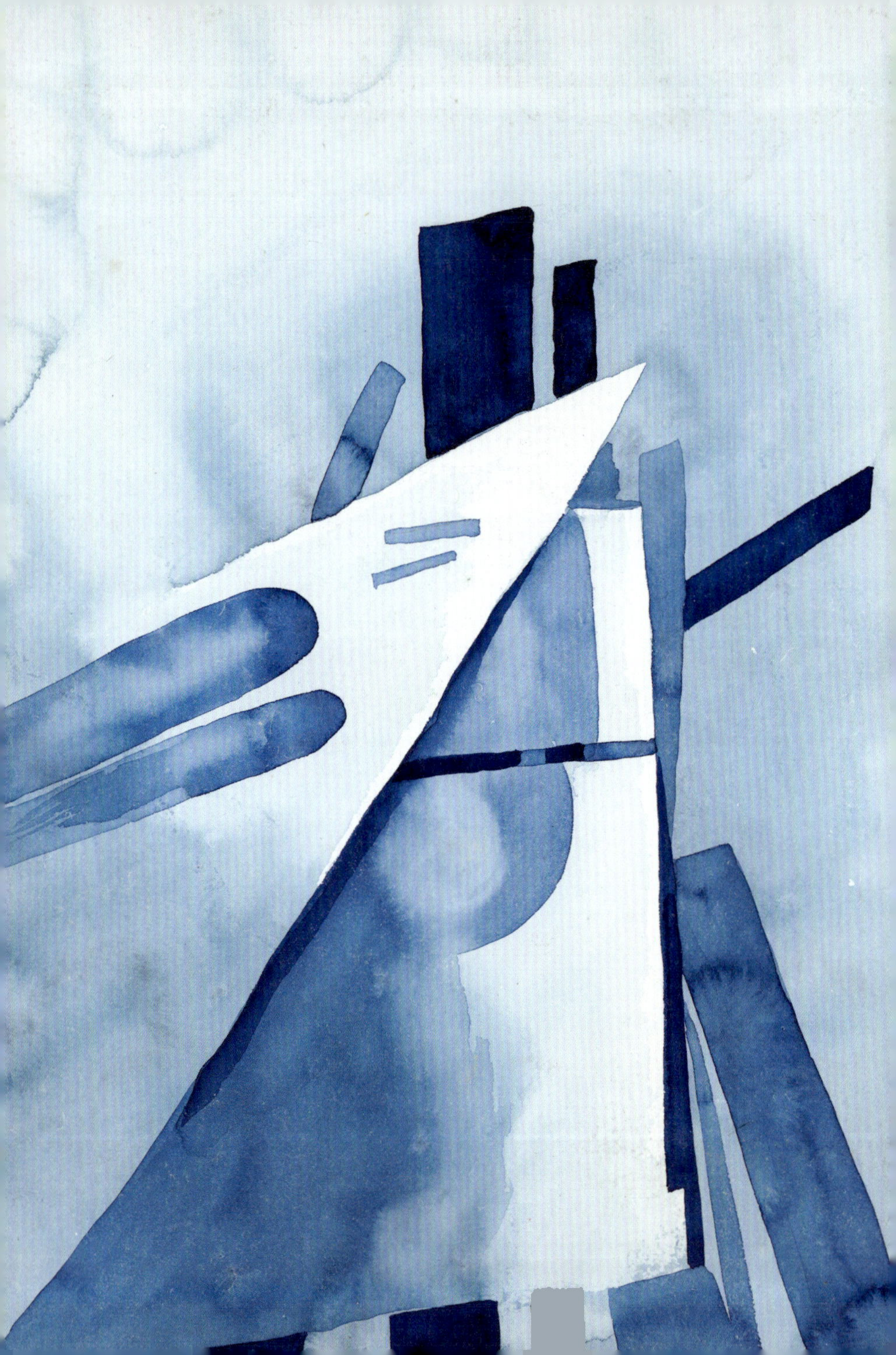

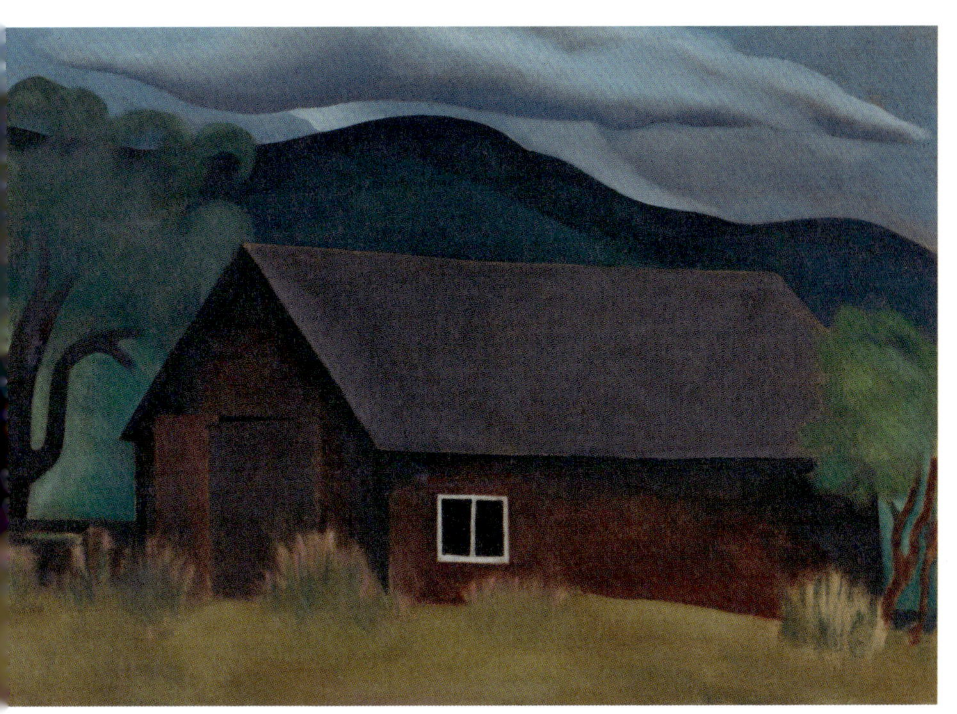

Blue Shapes 1919
Watercolour on paper
30.5 × 22.5

My Shanty, Lake George 1922
Oil paint on canvas
50.8 × 68.9

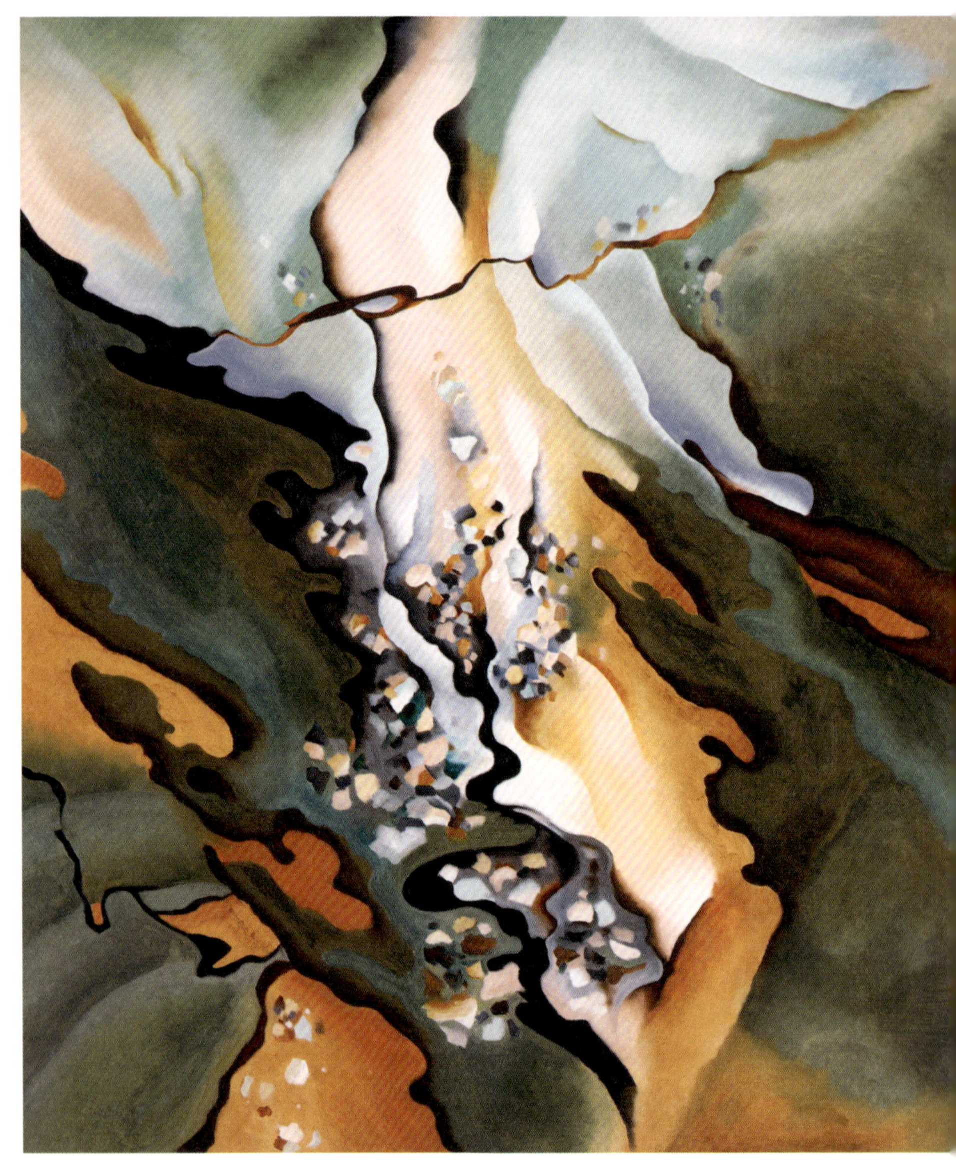

From the Lake No.3 1924
Oil paint on canvas
91.4 × 76.2

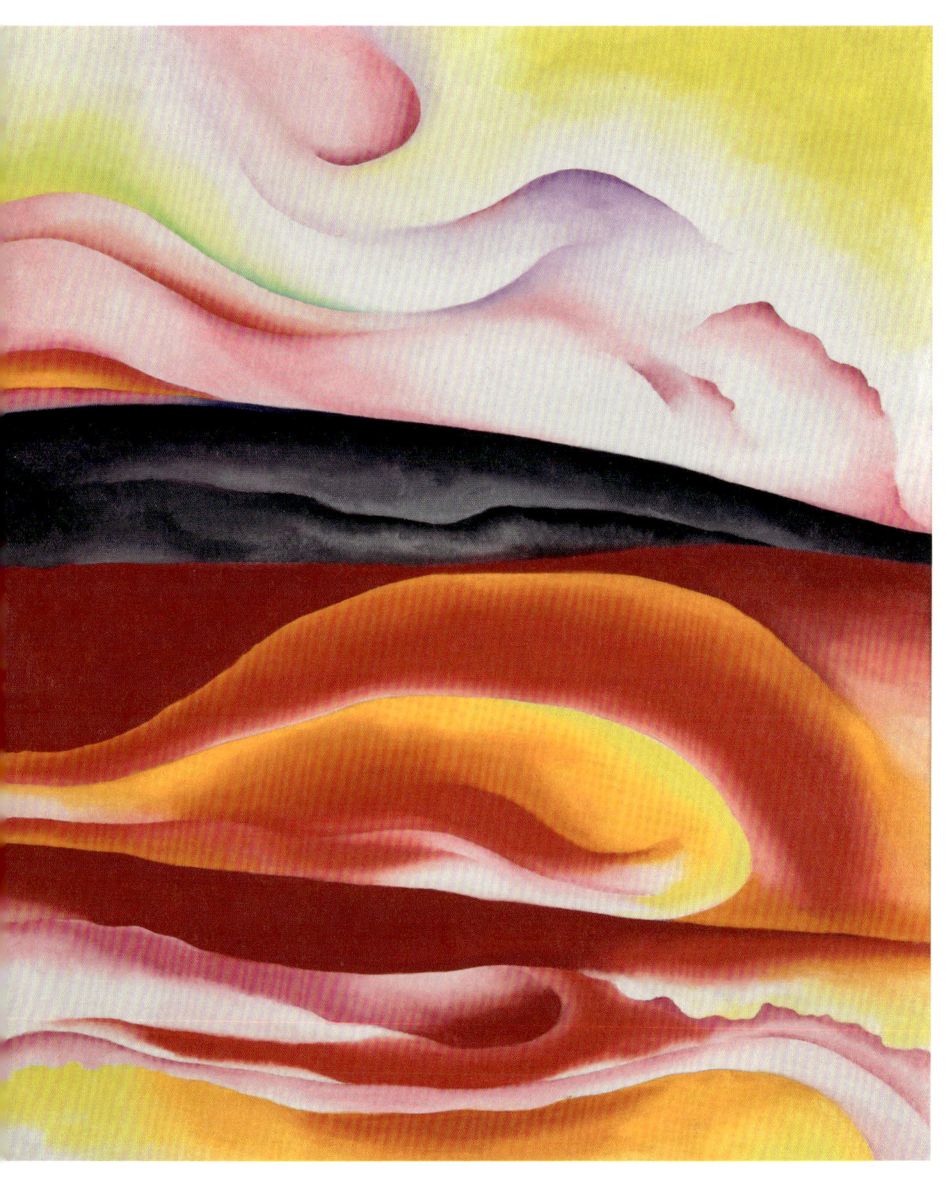

ed, Yellow and Black Streak
924
Dil paint on canvas
00.3 × 81.3

City Night 1926
Oil paint on canvas
121.9 × 76.2

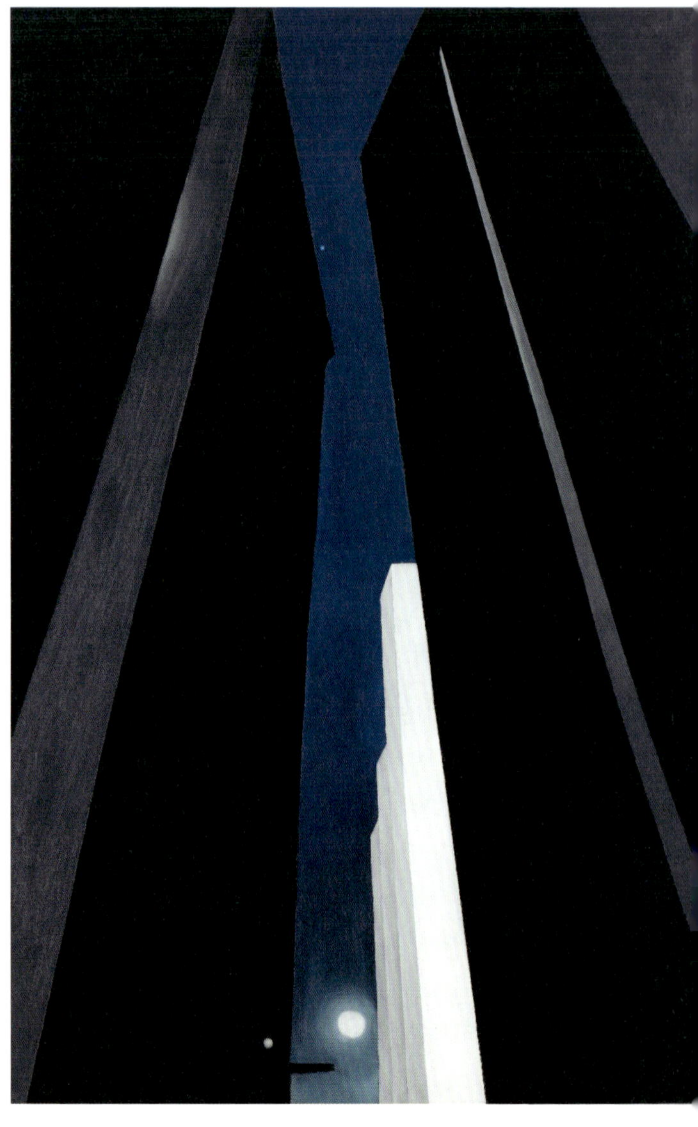

Radiator Building—Night, New York 1927
Oil paint on canvas
121.9 × 76.2

OVERLEAF
East River from the 30th Story of the Shelton Hotel 1928
Oil paint on canvas
76.8 × 121.9

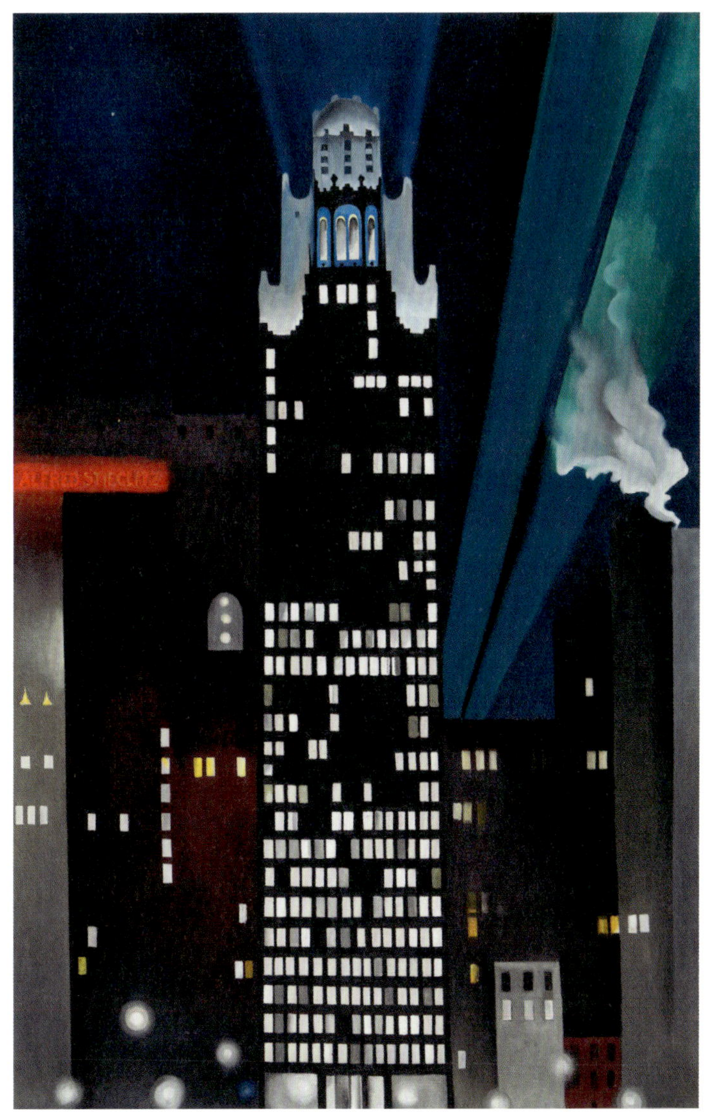

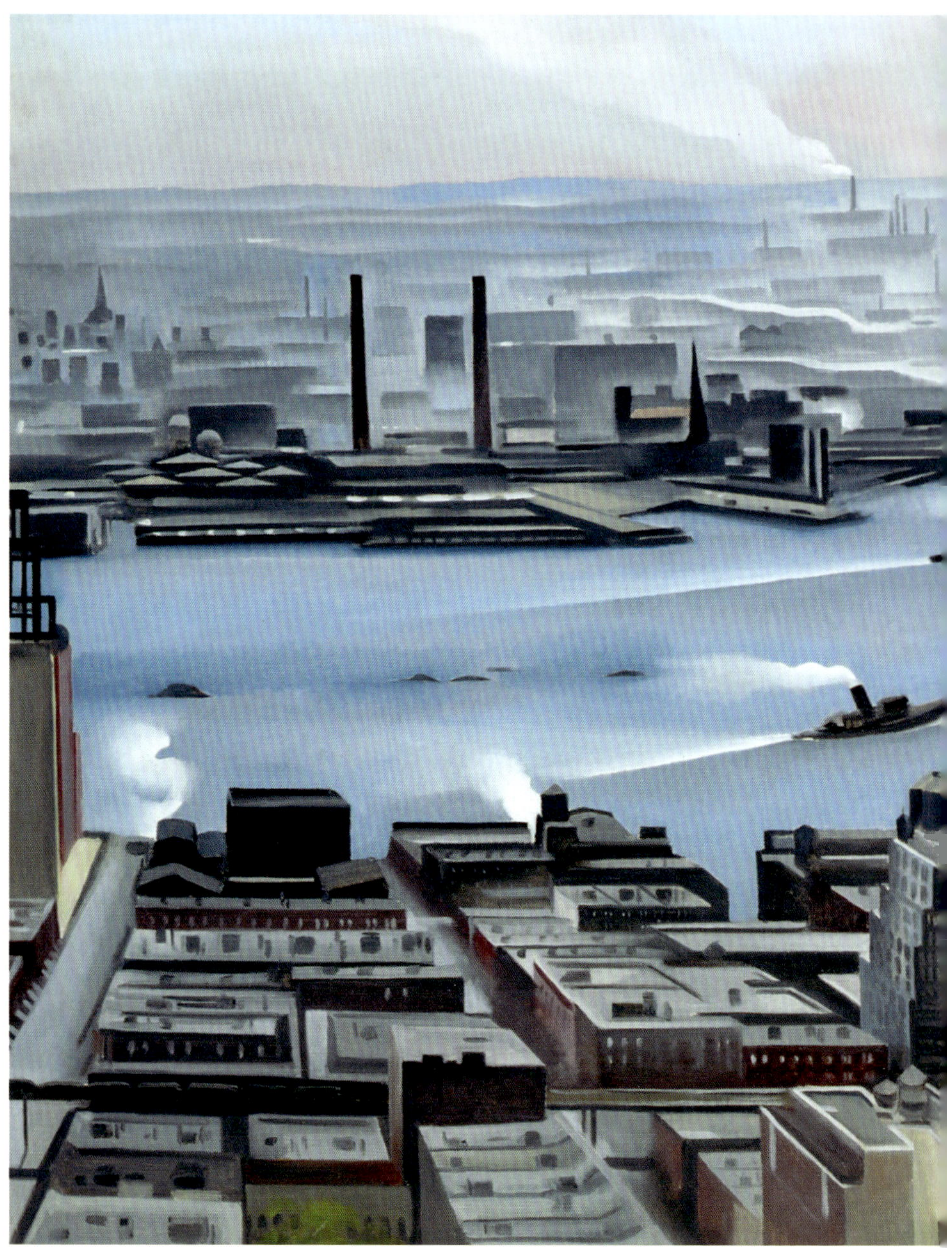

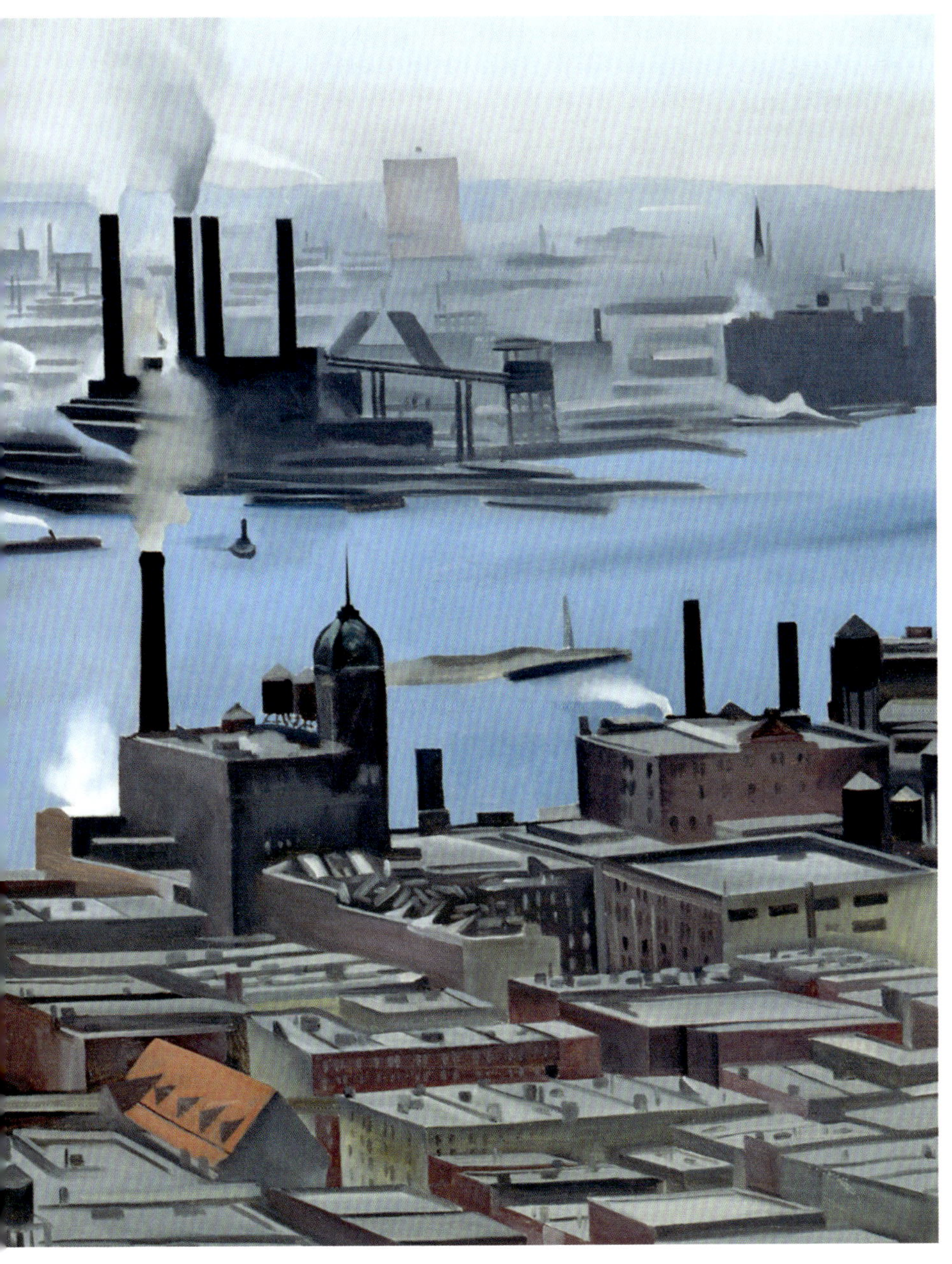

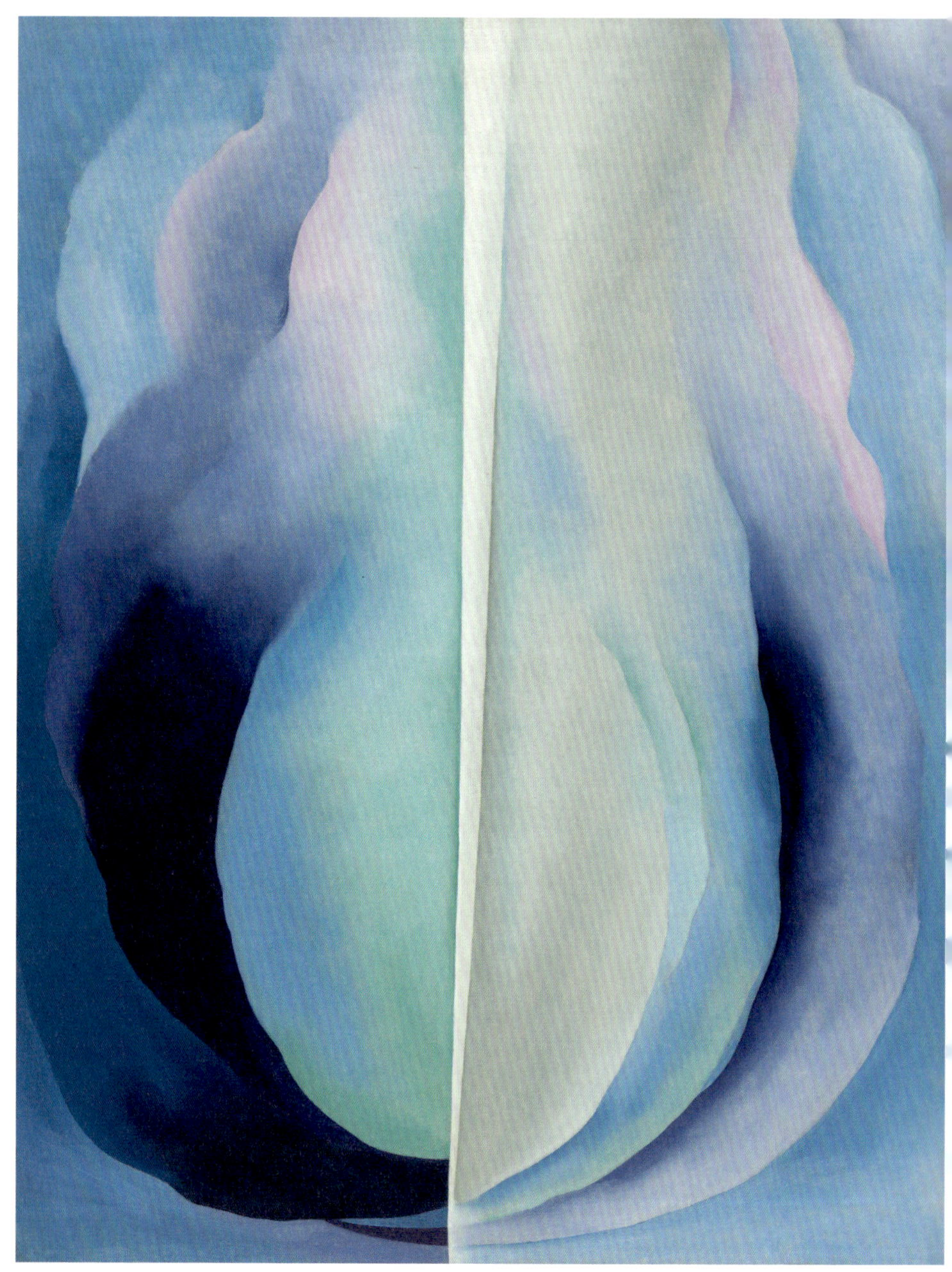

Abstraction Blue 1927
Oil paint on canvas
102.1 × 76

Dark Iris No.III 1927
Oil pastel on paper
51.4 × 22.9

OVERLEAF
Oriental Poppies 1927
Oil paint on canvas
76.2 × 101.9

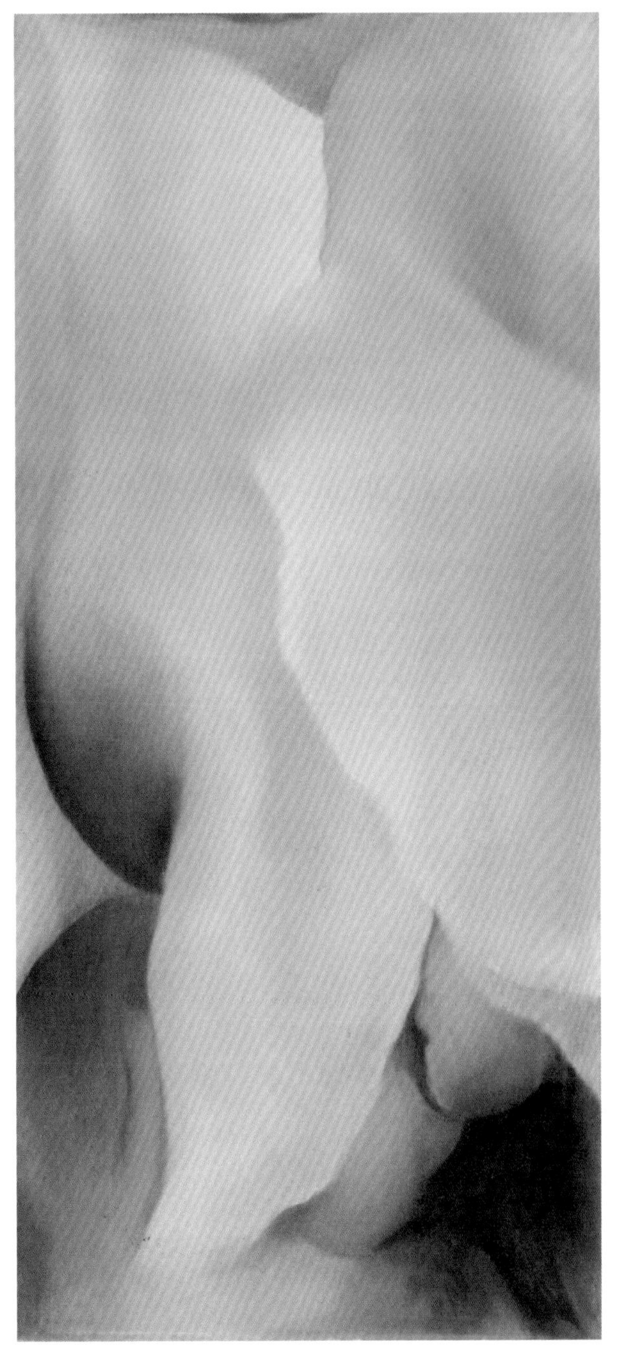

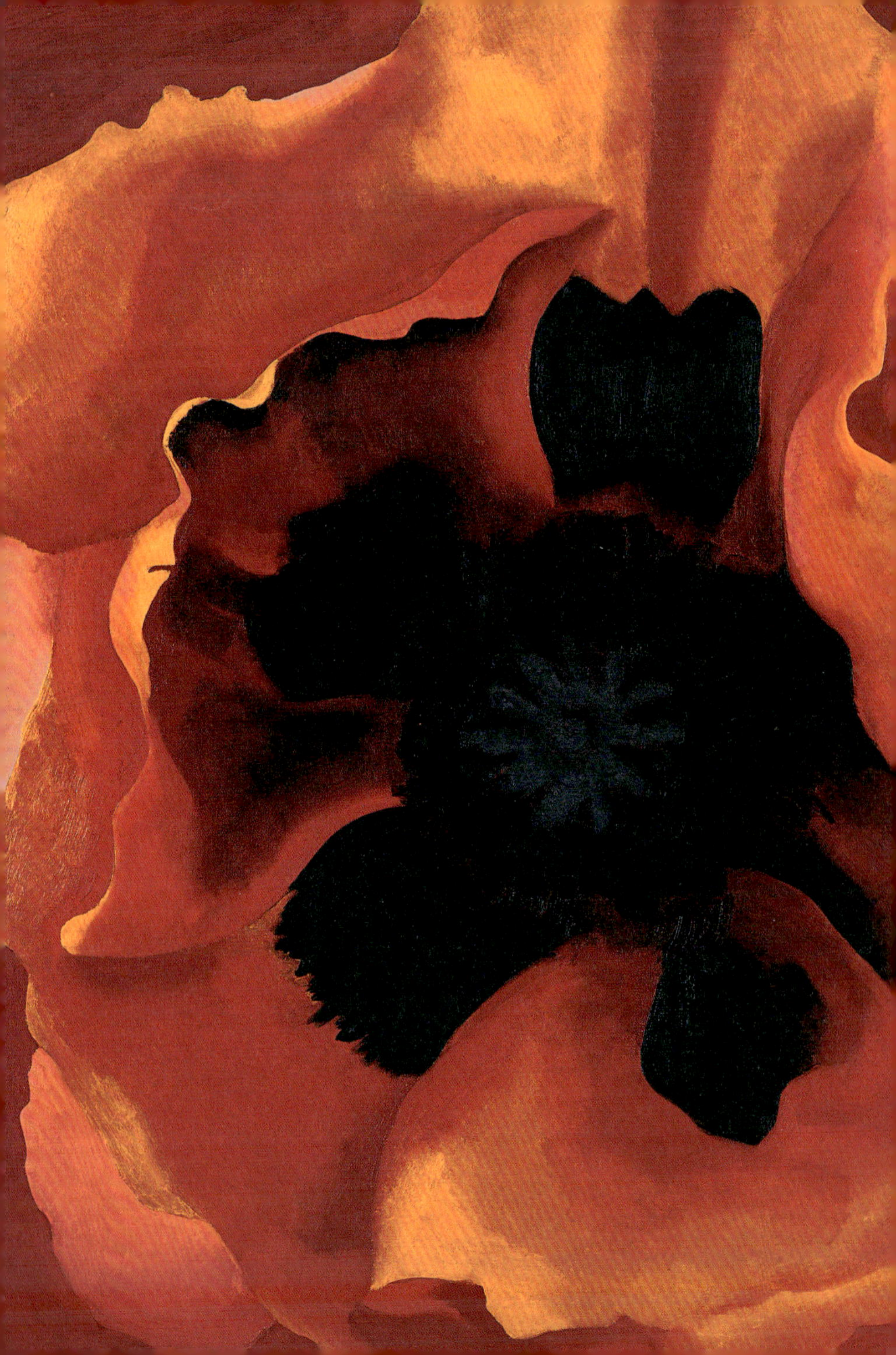

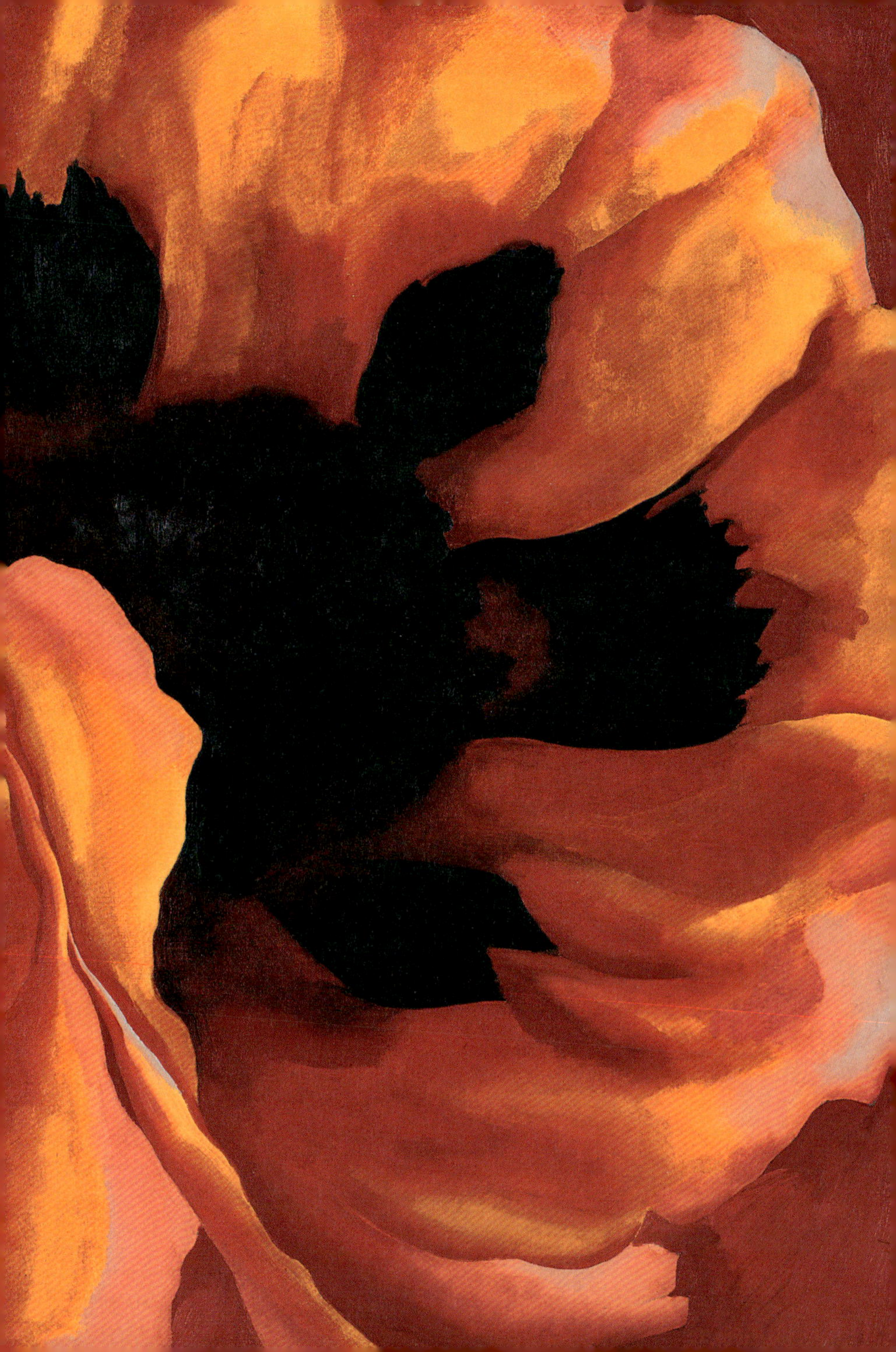

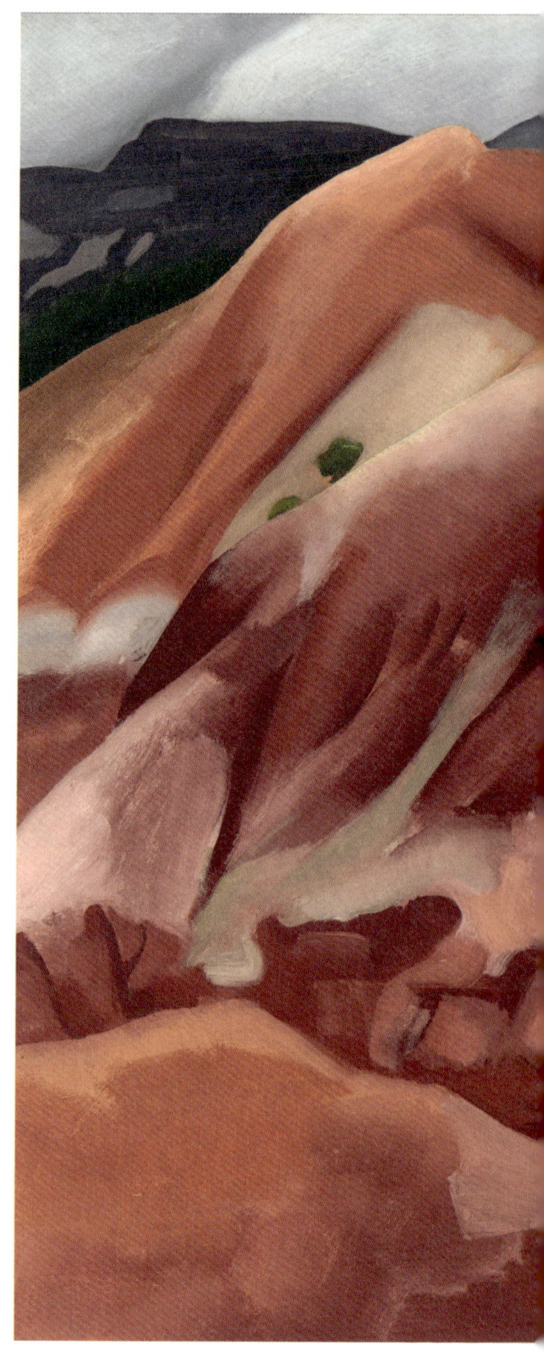

The Mountain, New Mexico
1931
Oil paint on canvas
76.4 × 91.8

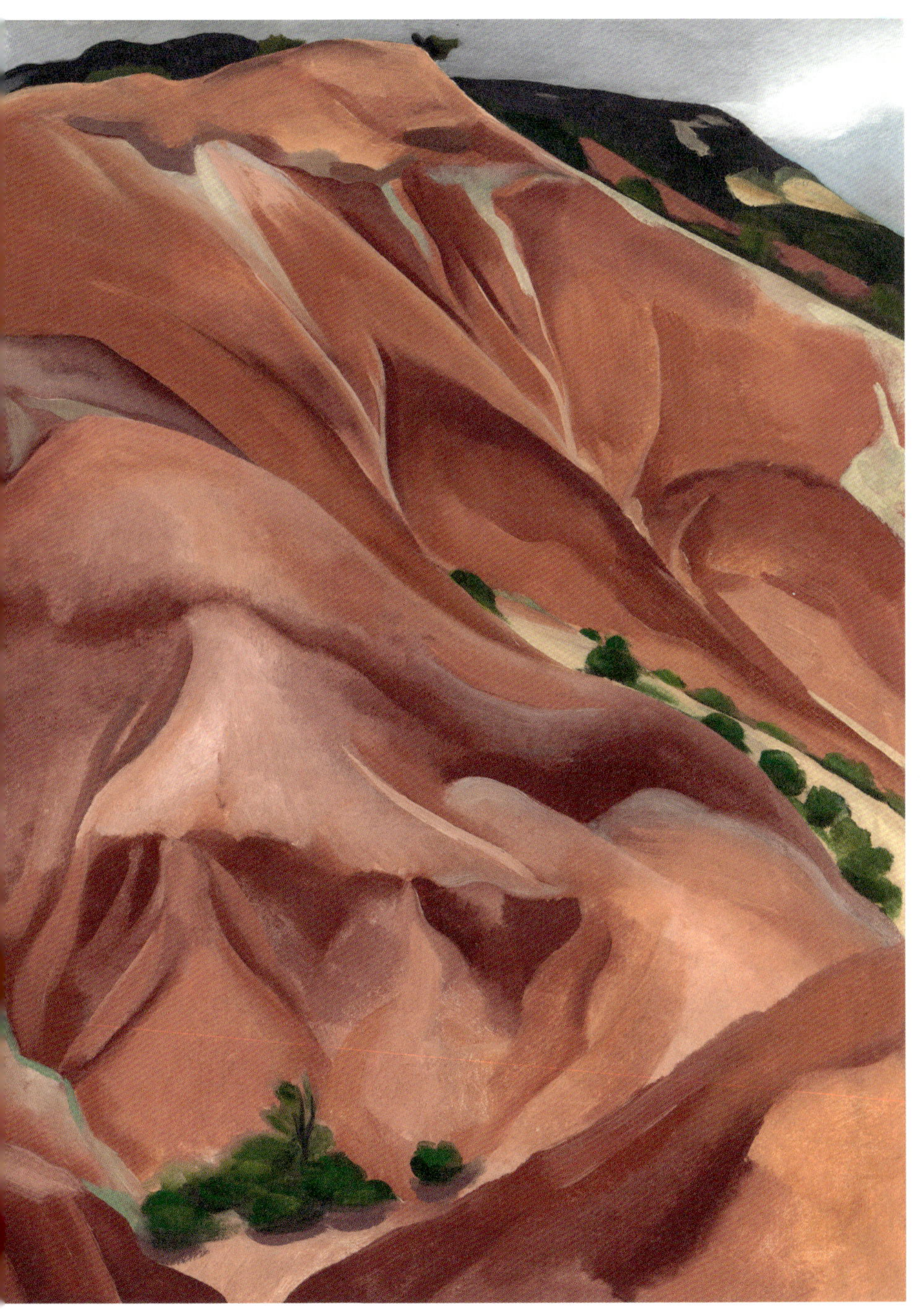

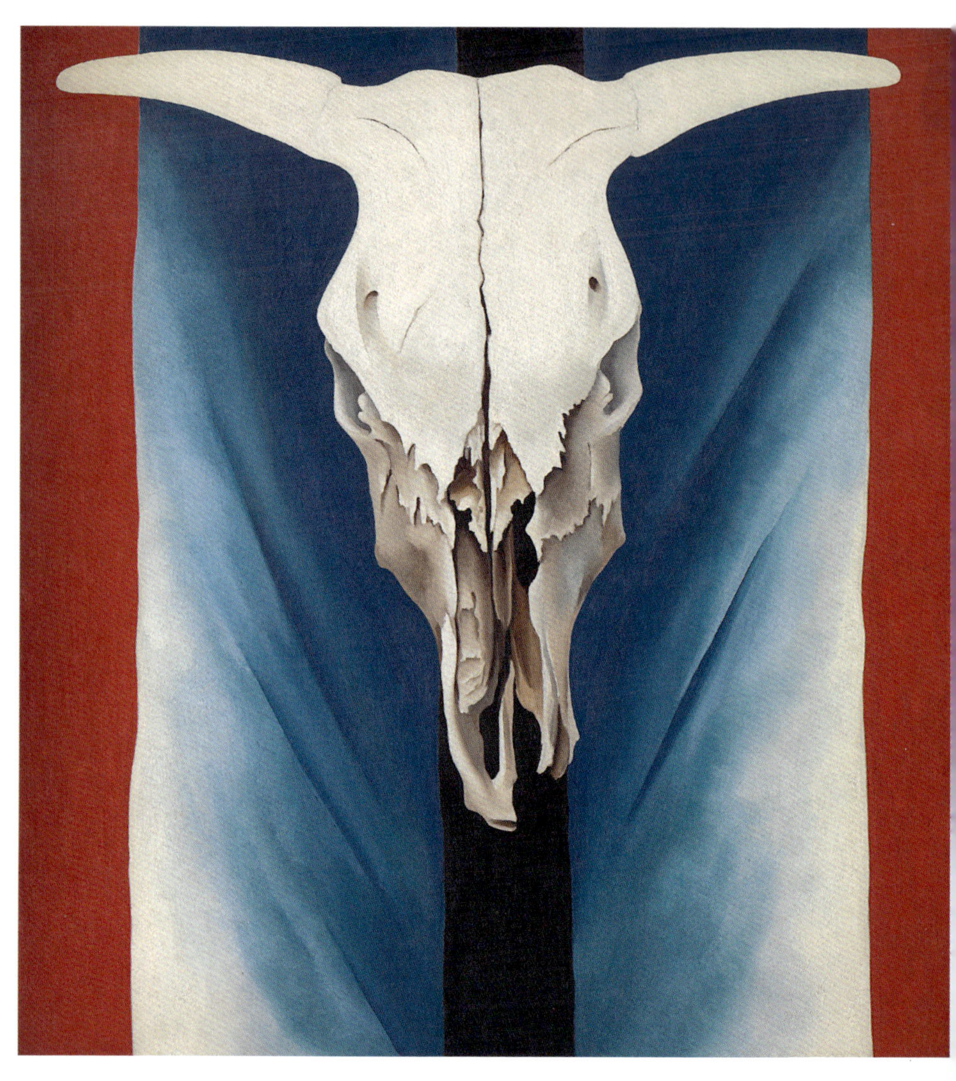

Cow's Skull, Red, White and Blue 1931
Oil paint on canvas
101.3 × 91.1

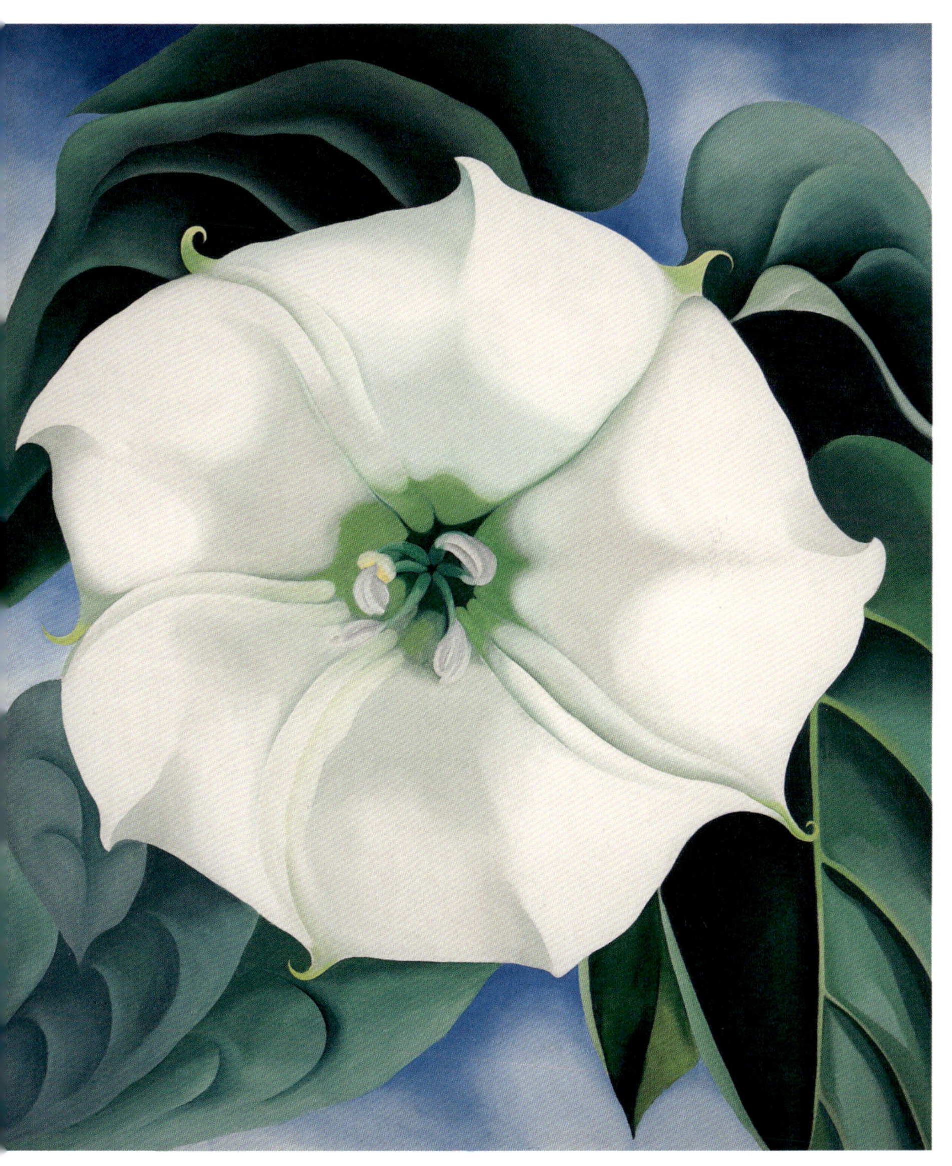

imson Weed/White Flower
No.1 1932
Dil paint on canvas
21.9 × 101.6

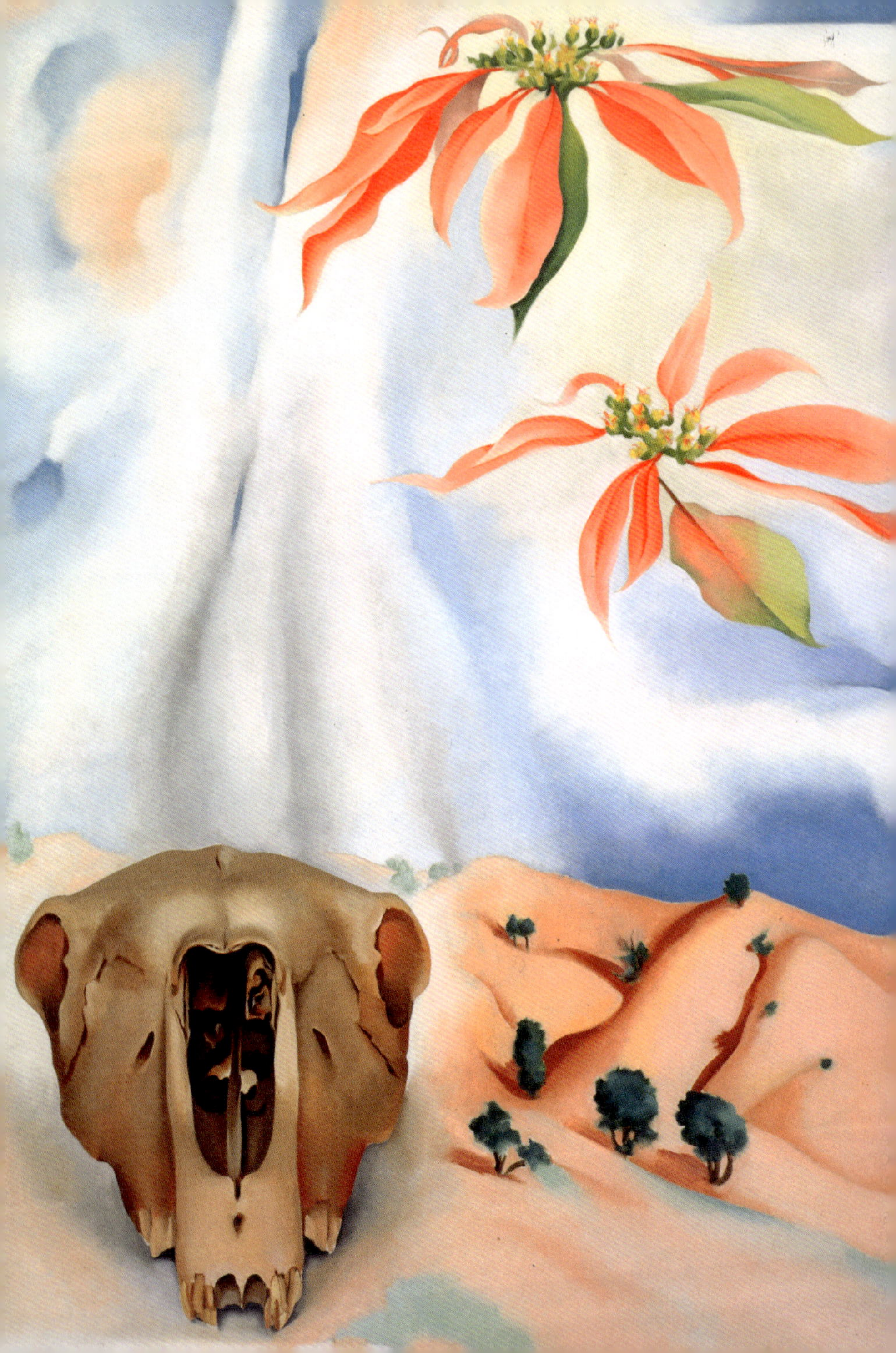

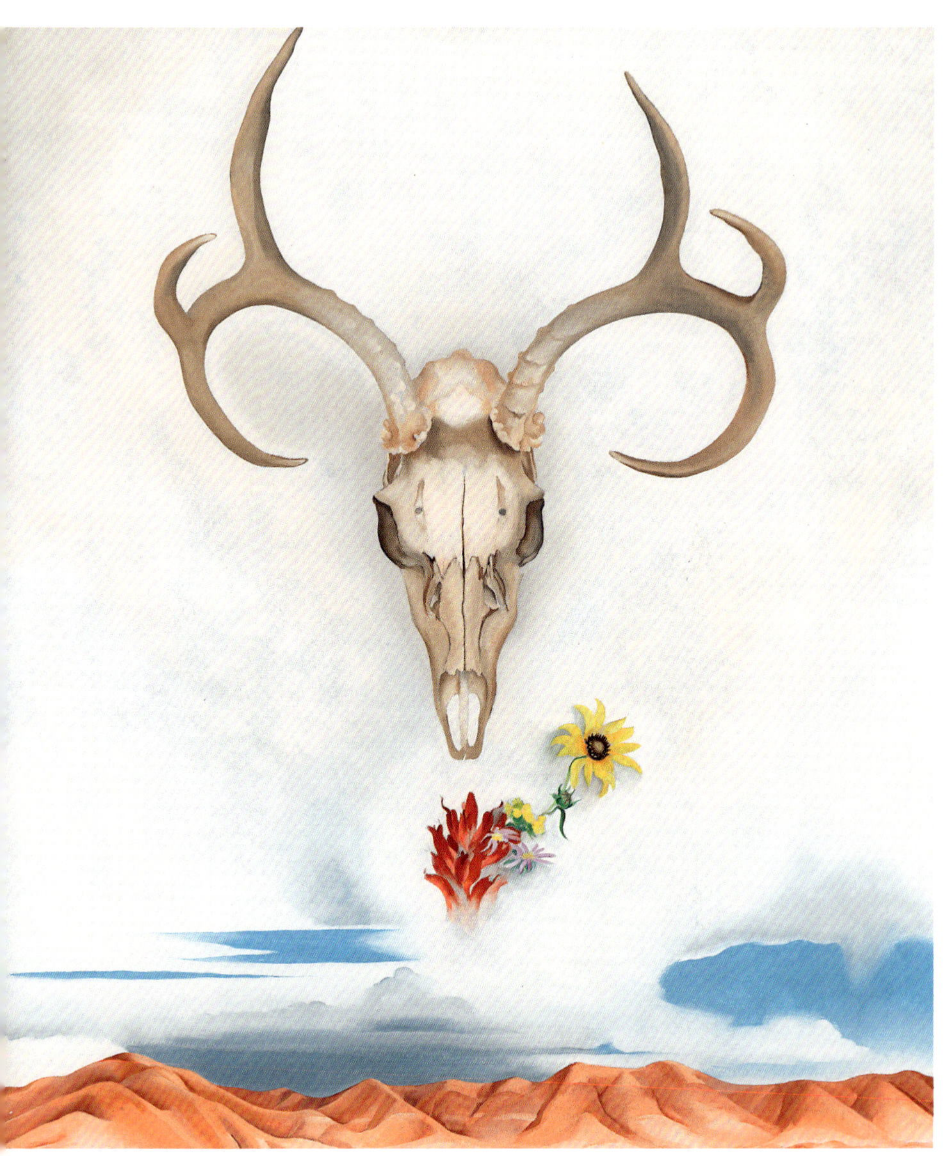

Mule's Skull with Pink Poinsettia 1936
Oil paint on canvas
101.9 × 76.2

Summer Days 1936
Oil paint on canvas
91.8 × 76.5

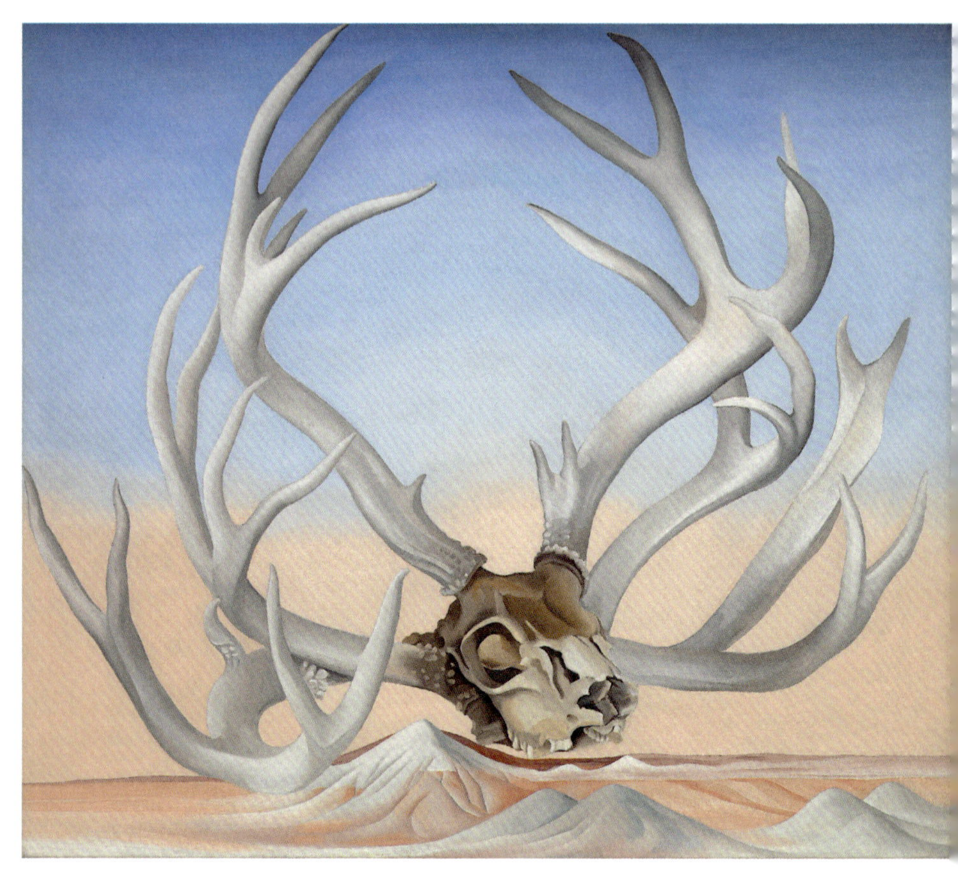

From the Faraway, Nearby 1937
Oil paint on canvas
91.4 × 101.9

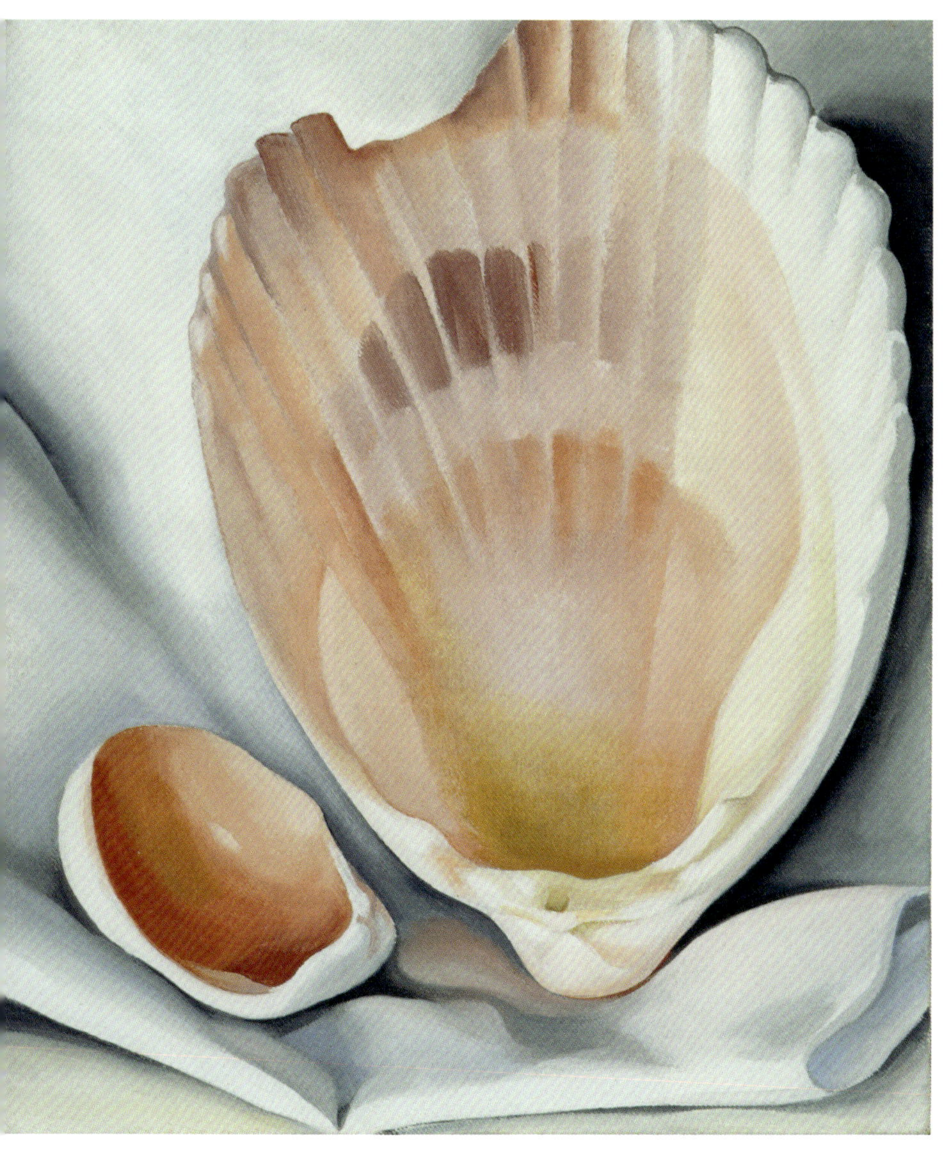

Two Pink Shells/Pink Shell 1937
Oil paint on canvas
30.5 × 25.4

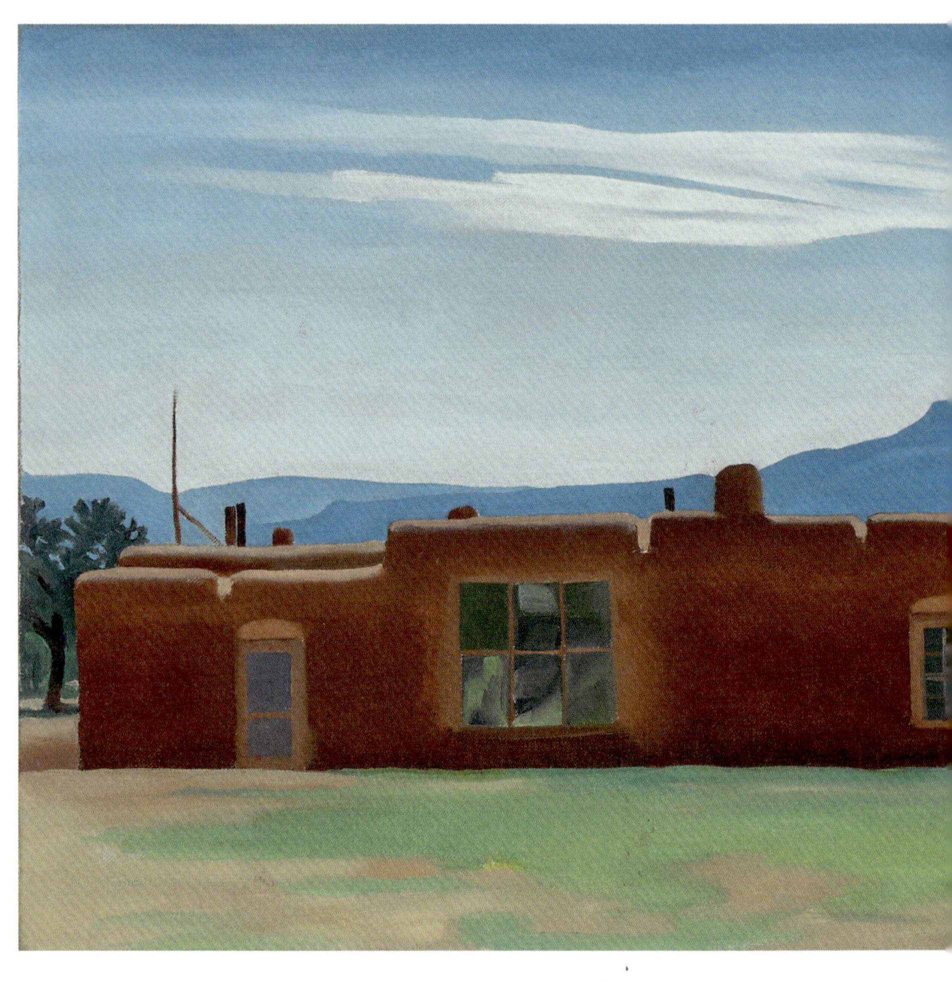

The House I Live In 1937
Oil paint on canvas
35.6 × 76.2

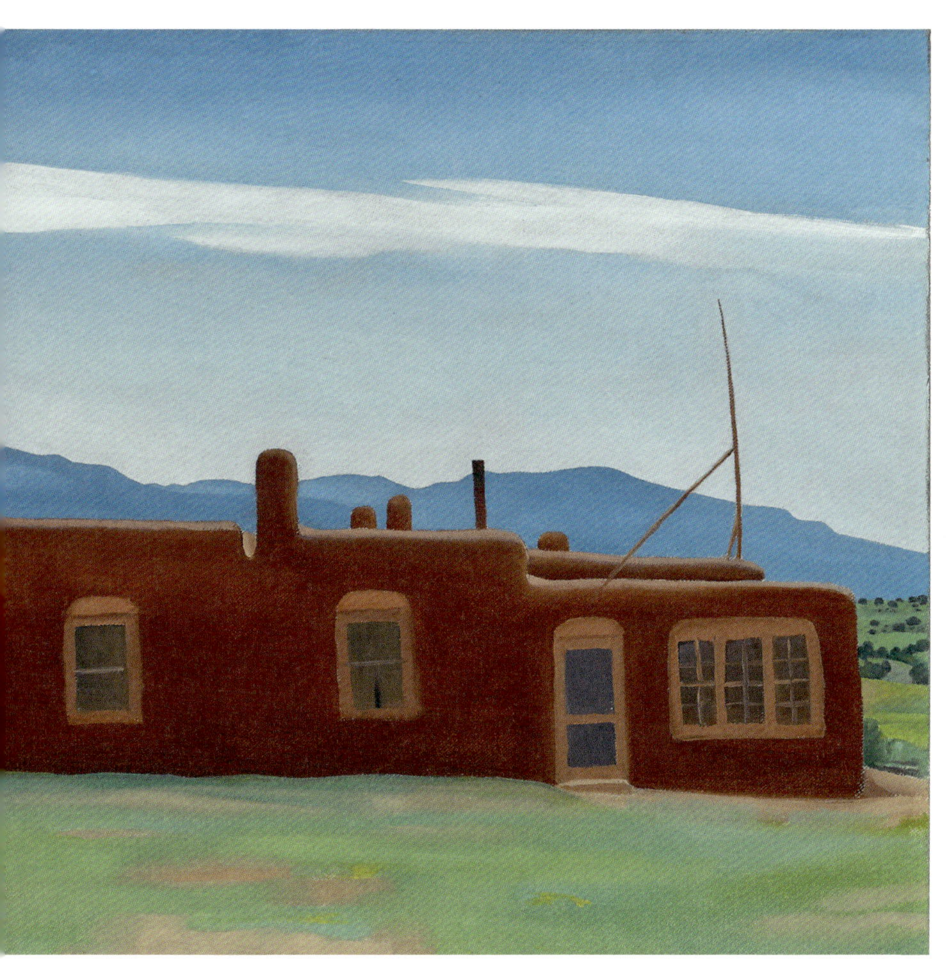

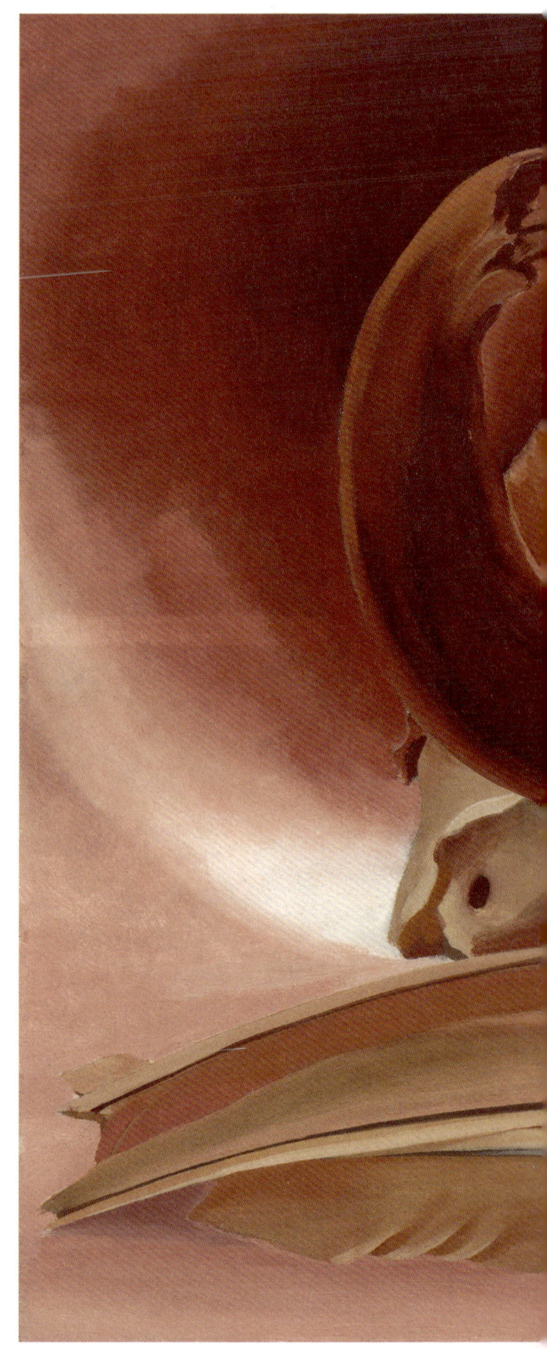

Horn and Feathers 1937
Oil paint on canvas
50.9 × 61.4

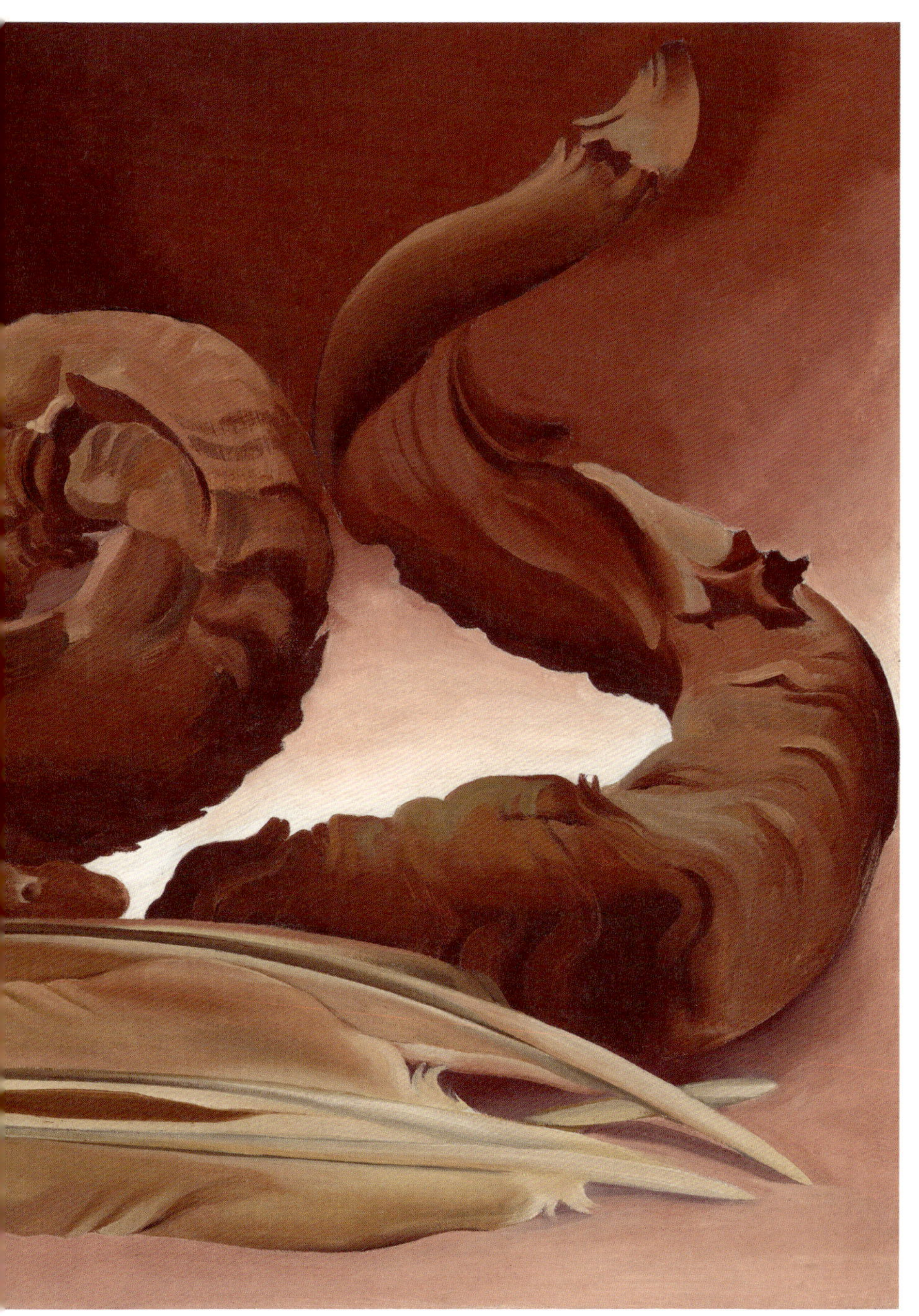

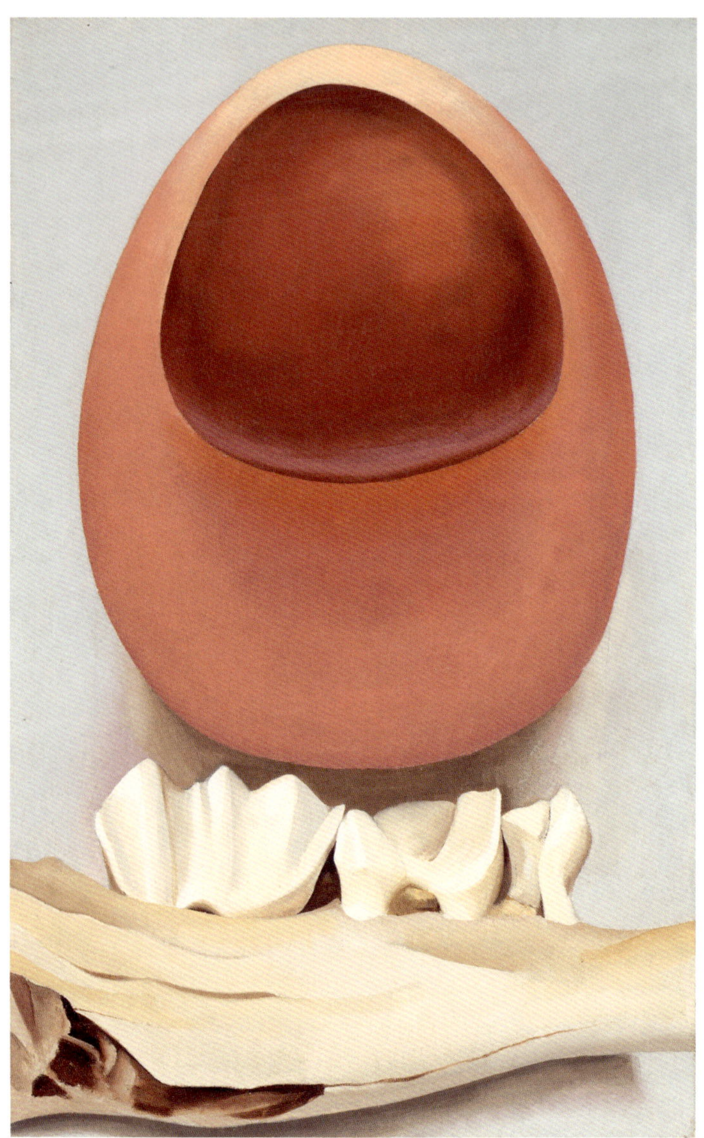

Red and Pink Rocks and Teeth
1938
Oil paint on canvas
53.3 × 33

Leaves of a Plant 1942
Oil paint on canvas
101.6 × 76.2

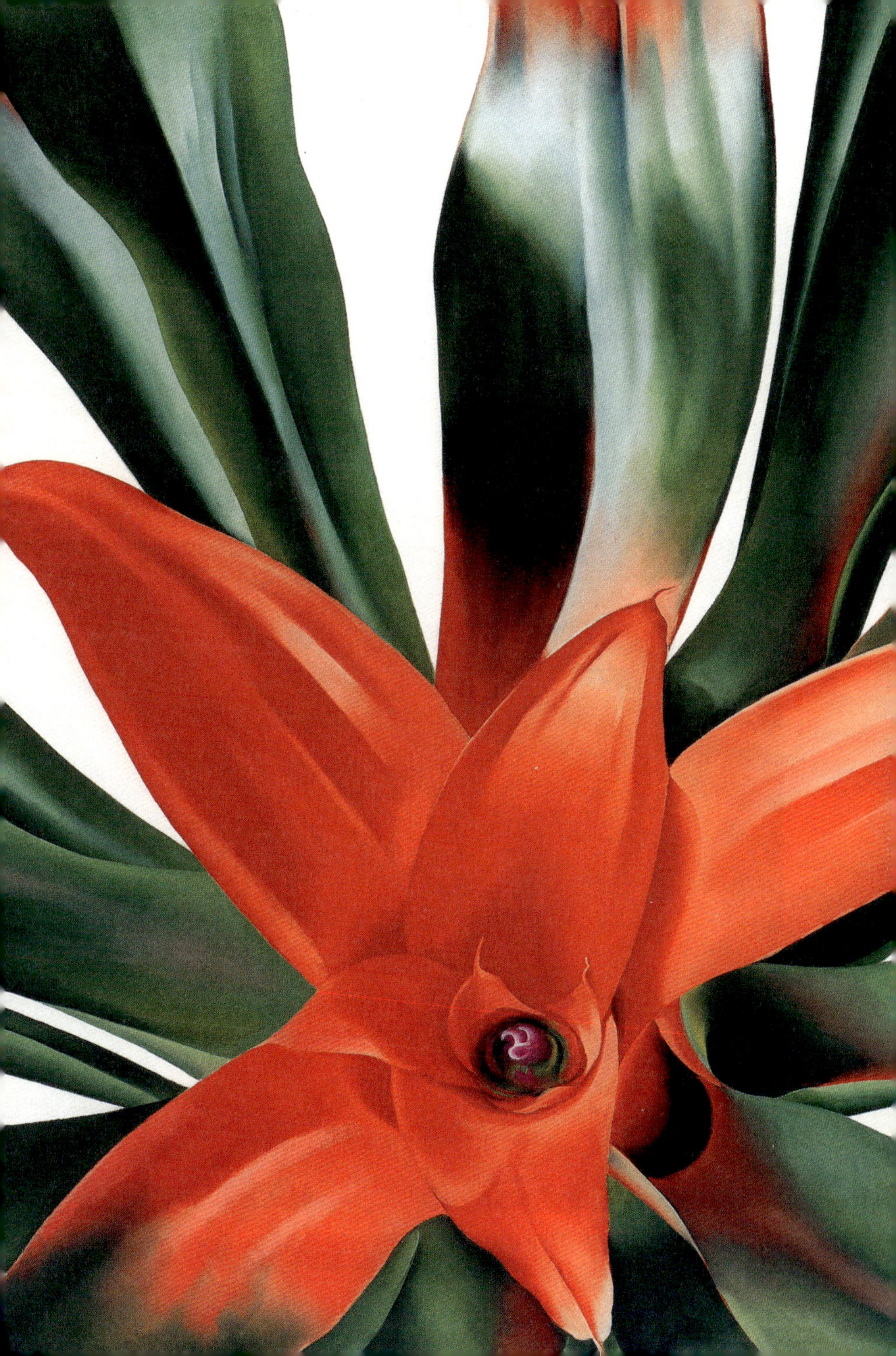

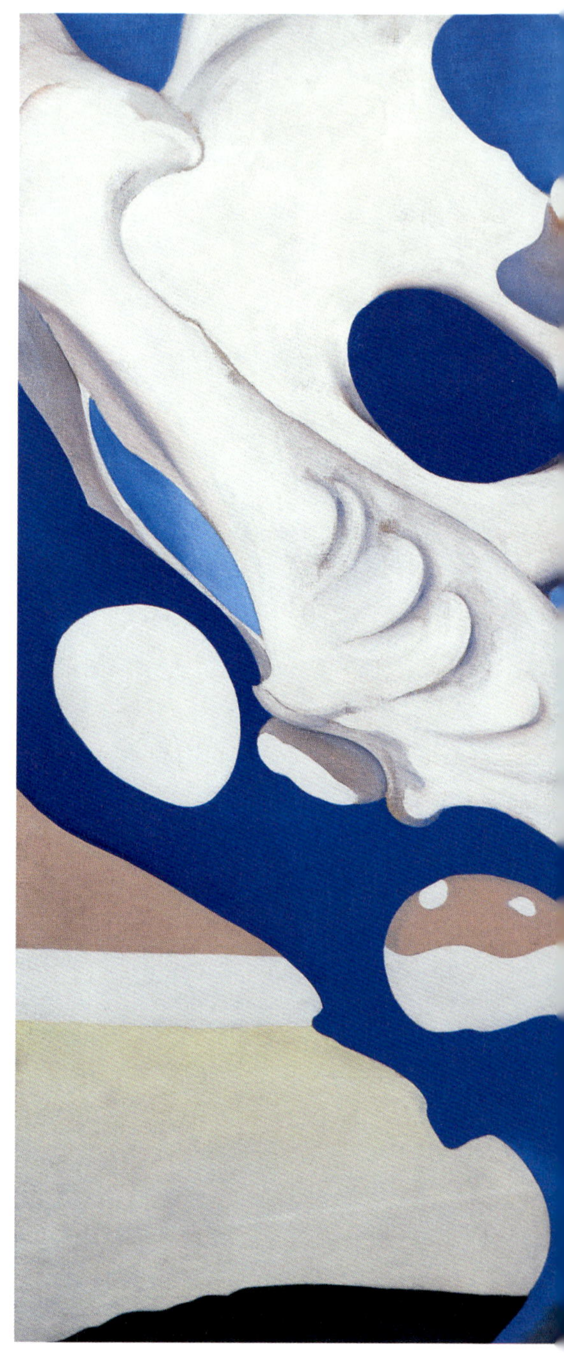

Pelvis with Shadows and the Moon 1943
Oil paint on canvas
101.6 × 123.8

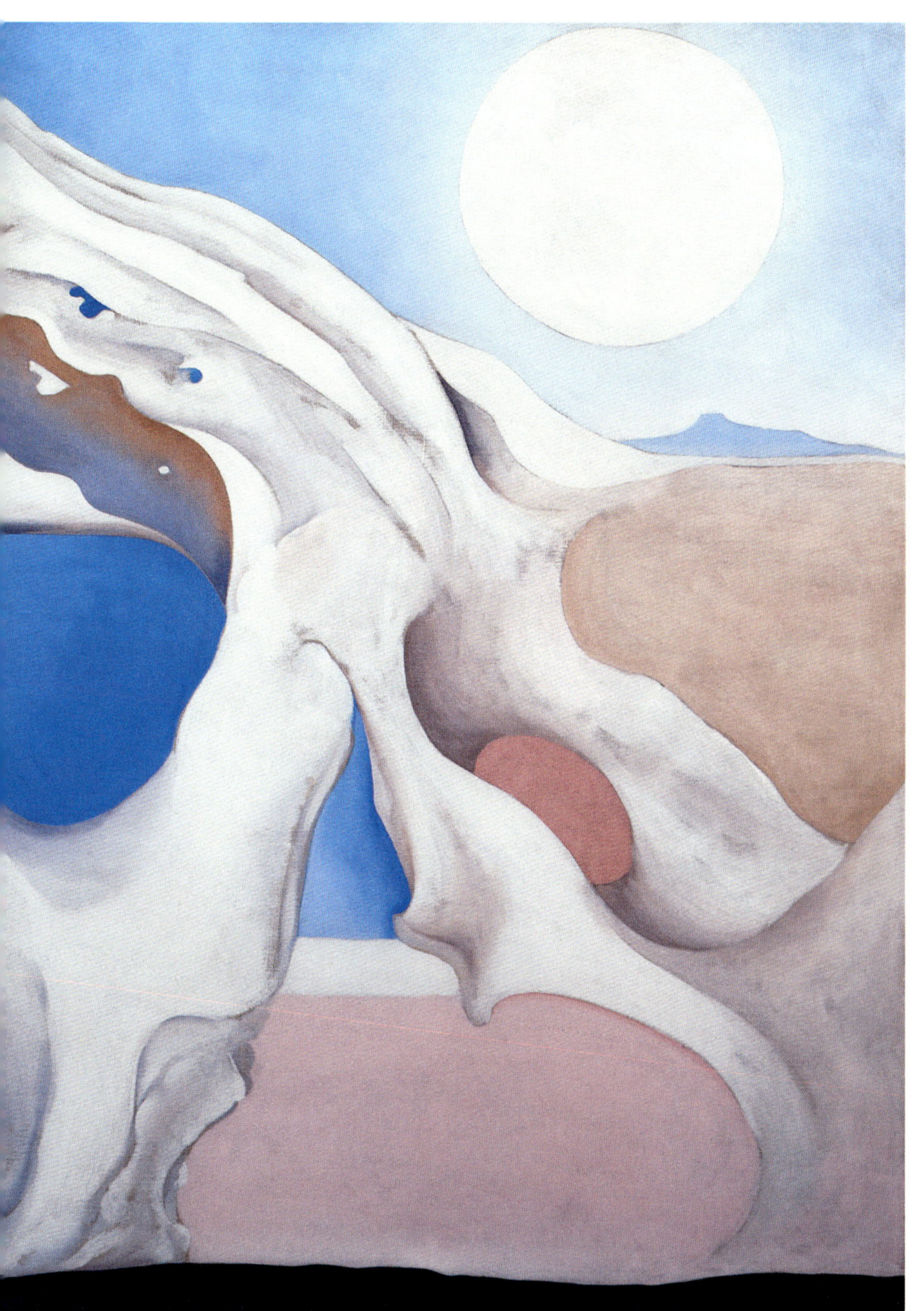

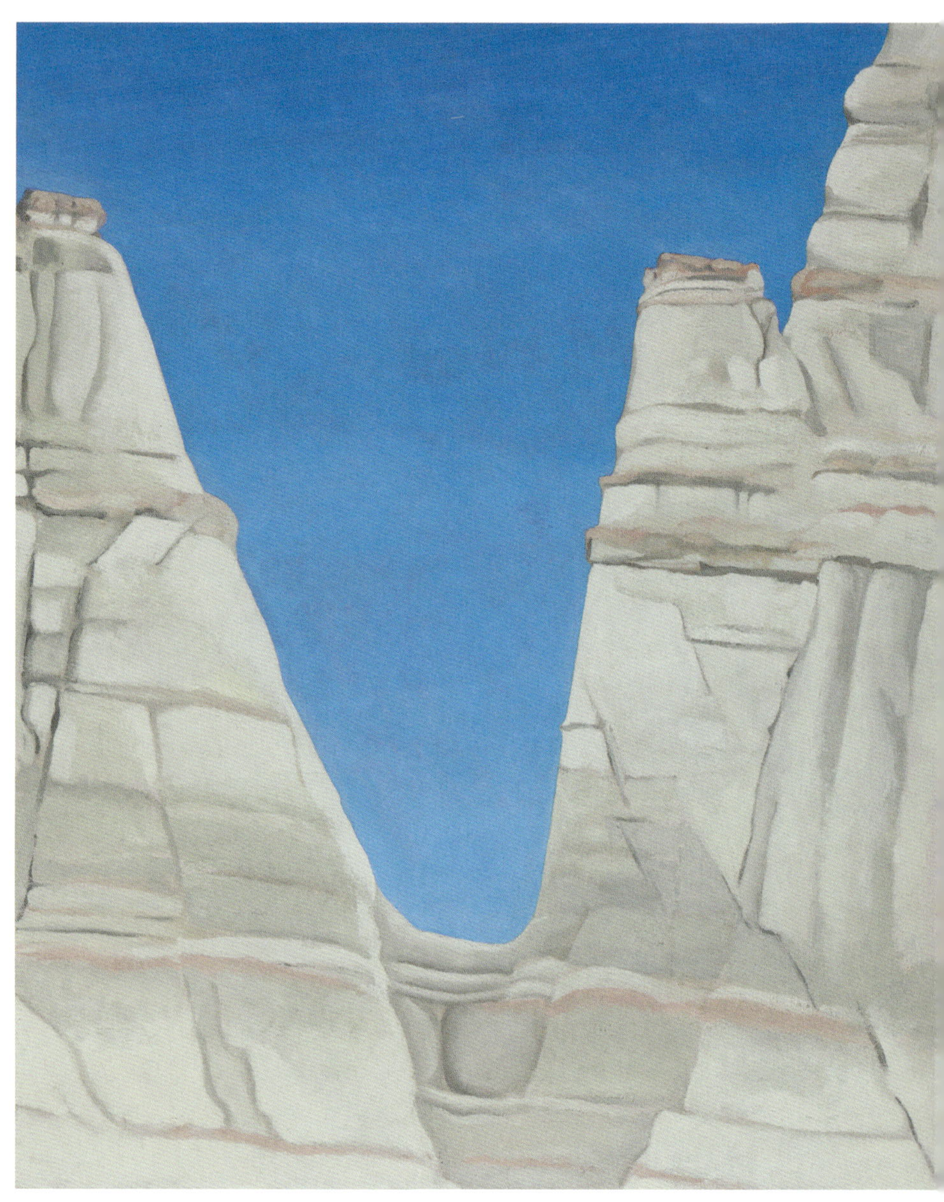

The White Place in Sun 1943
Oil paint on canvas
71.1 × 55.9

Black Place I 1945
Oil paint on canvas
75.25 × 90.65

OVERLEAF
Pelvis Series, Red with Yellow
1945
Oil paint on canvas
91.4 × 121.9

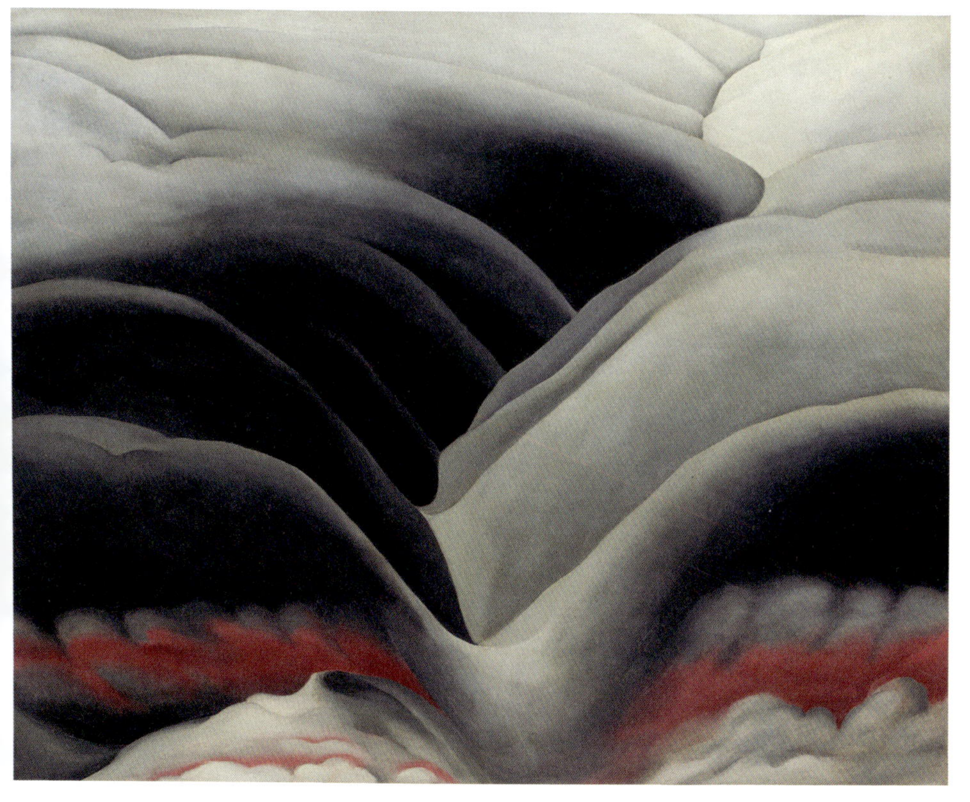

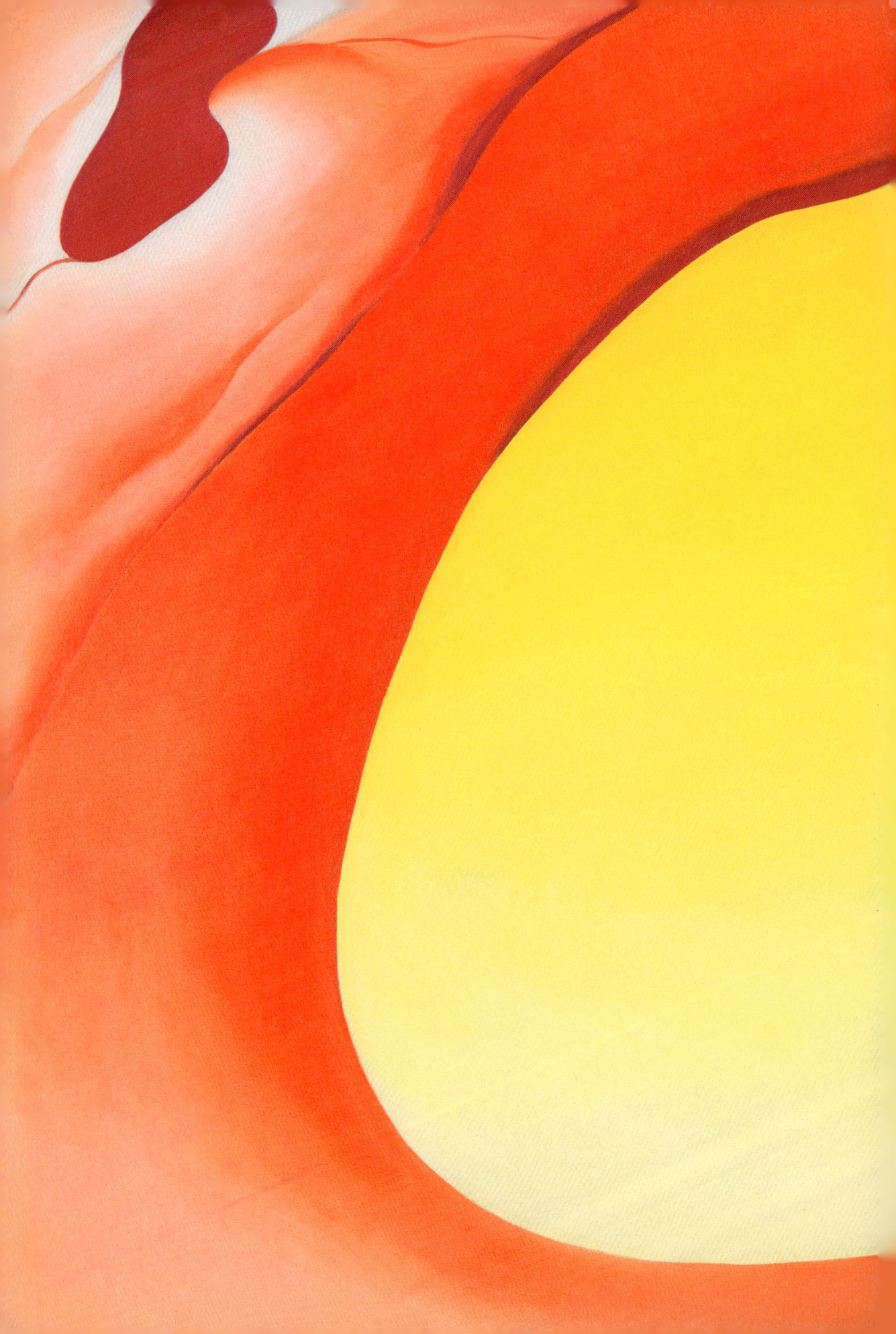

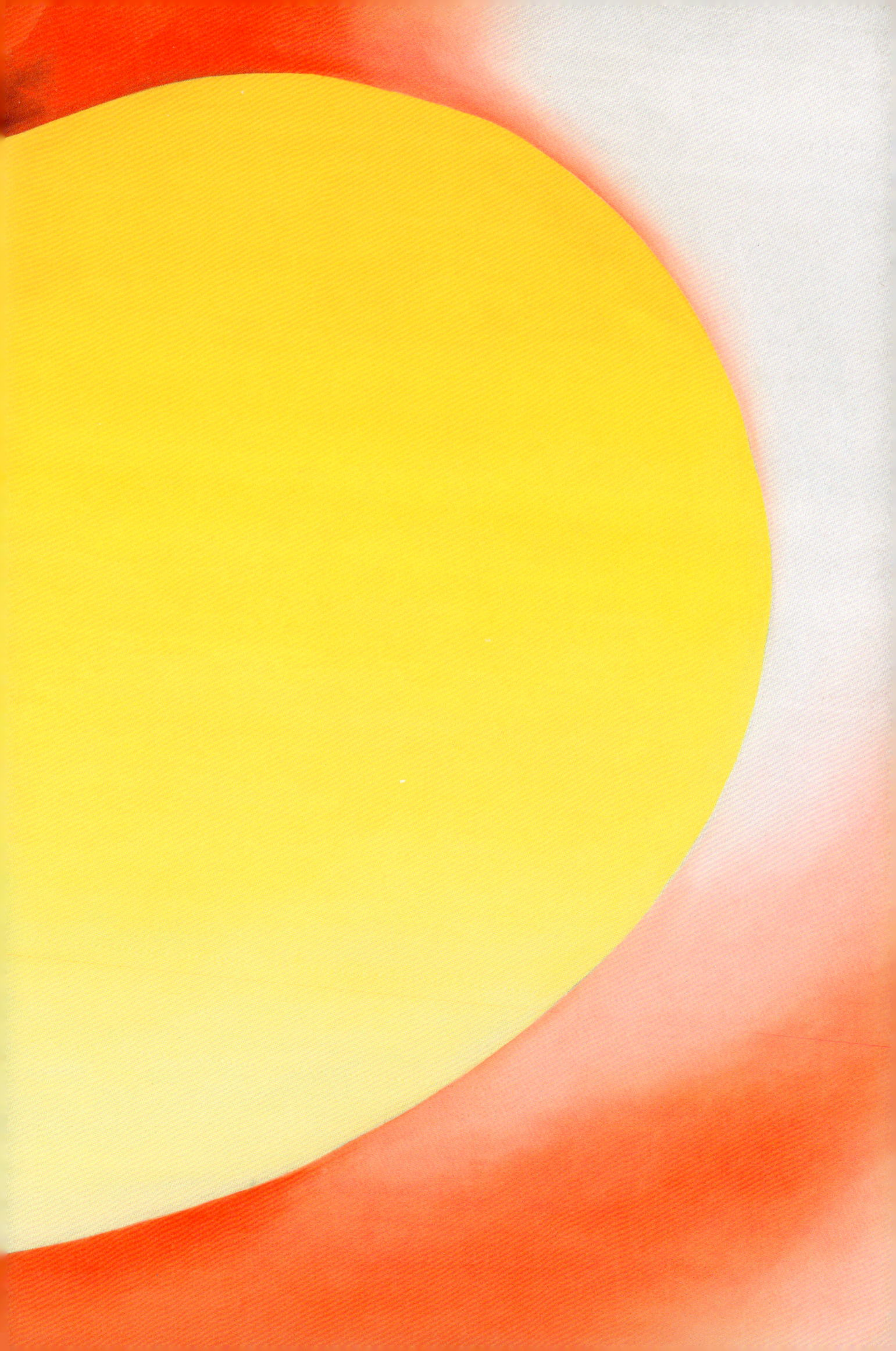

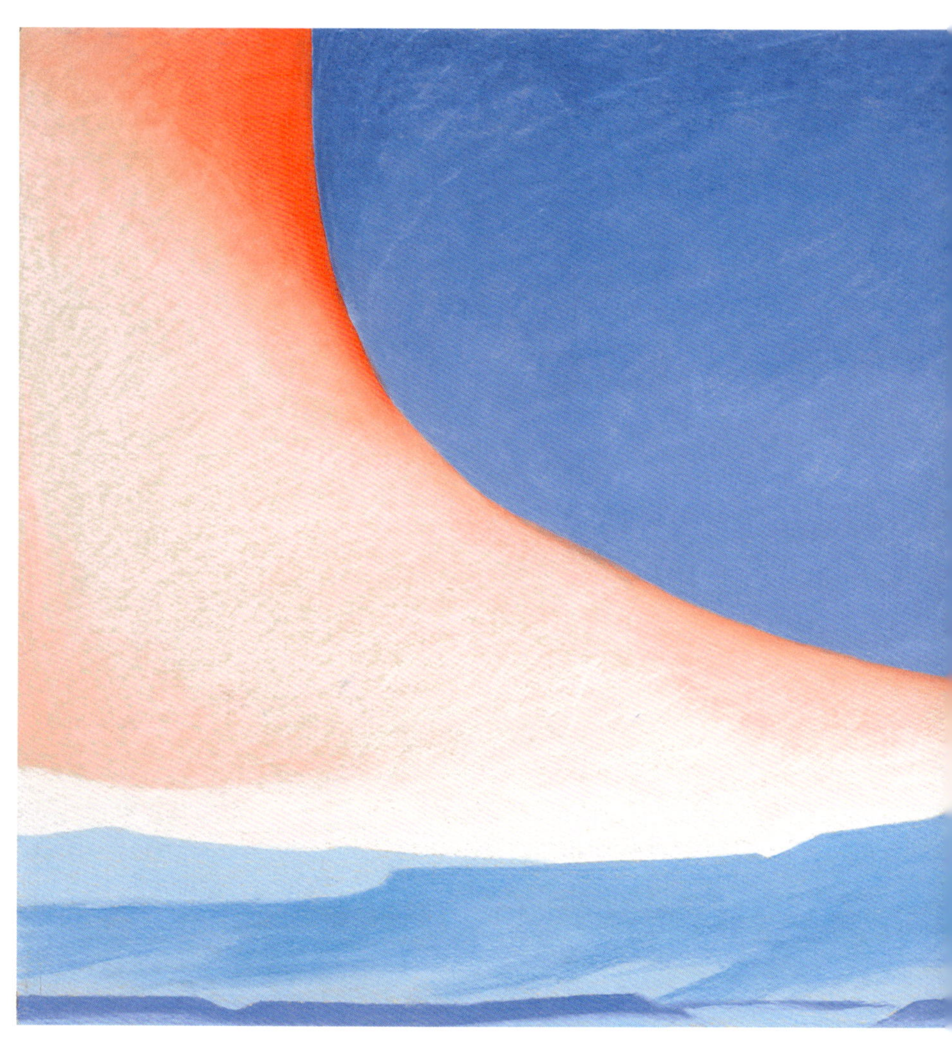

Pedernal 1945
Oil pastel on paper
54.3 × 109

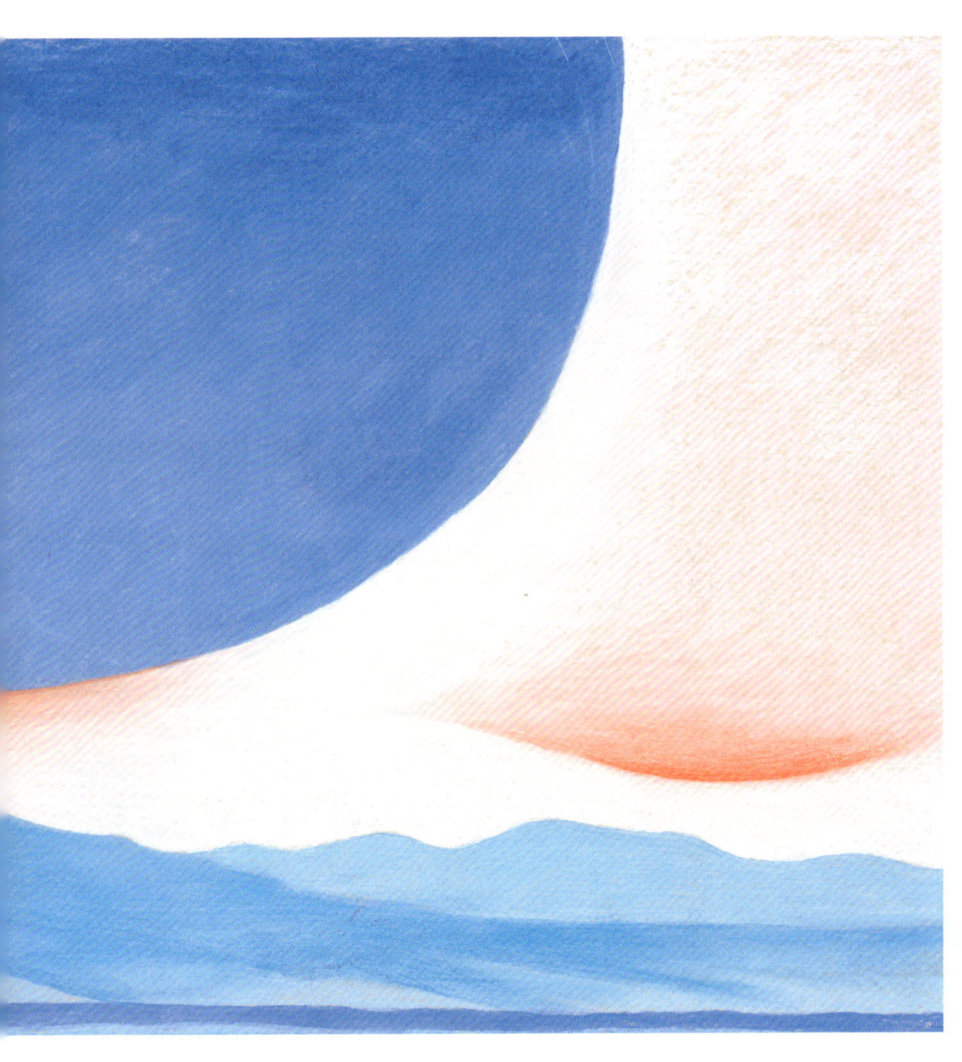

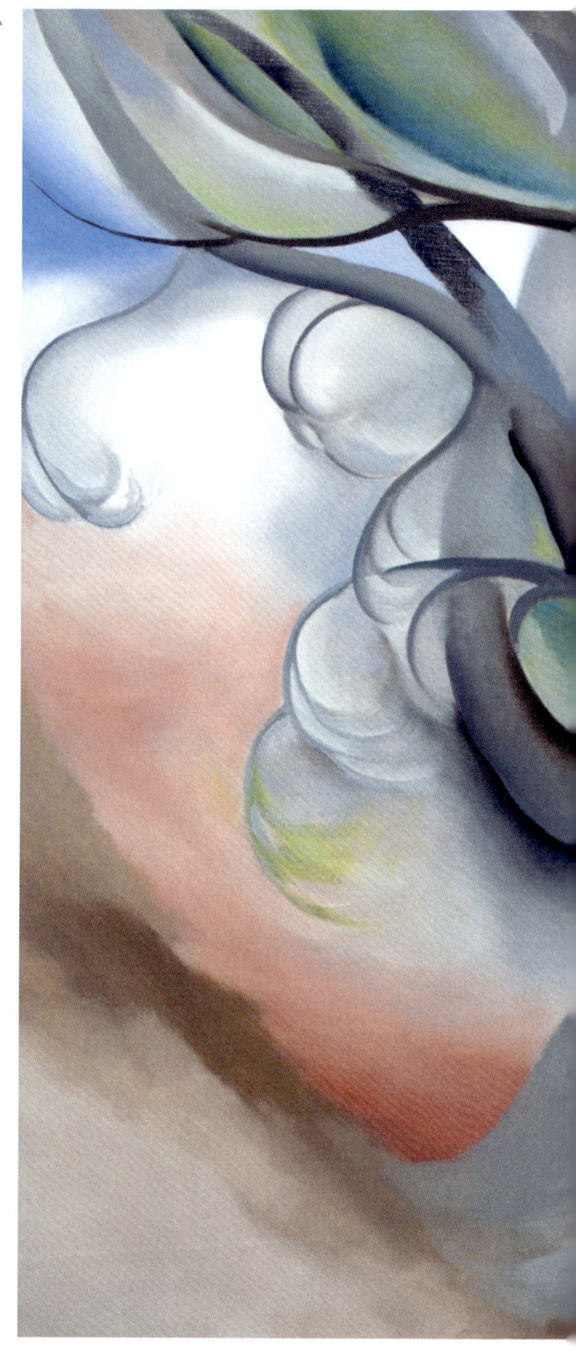

Spring Tree No.II 1945
Oil paint on canvas
76.2 × 91.4

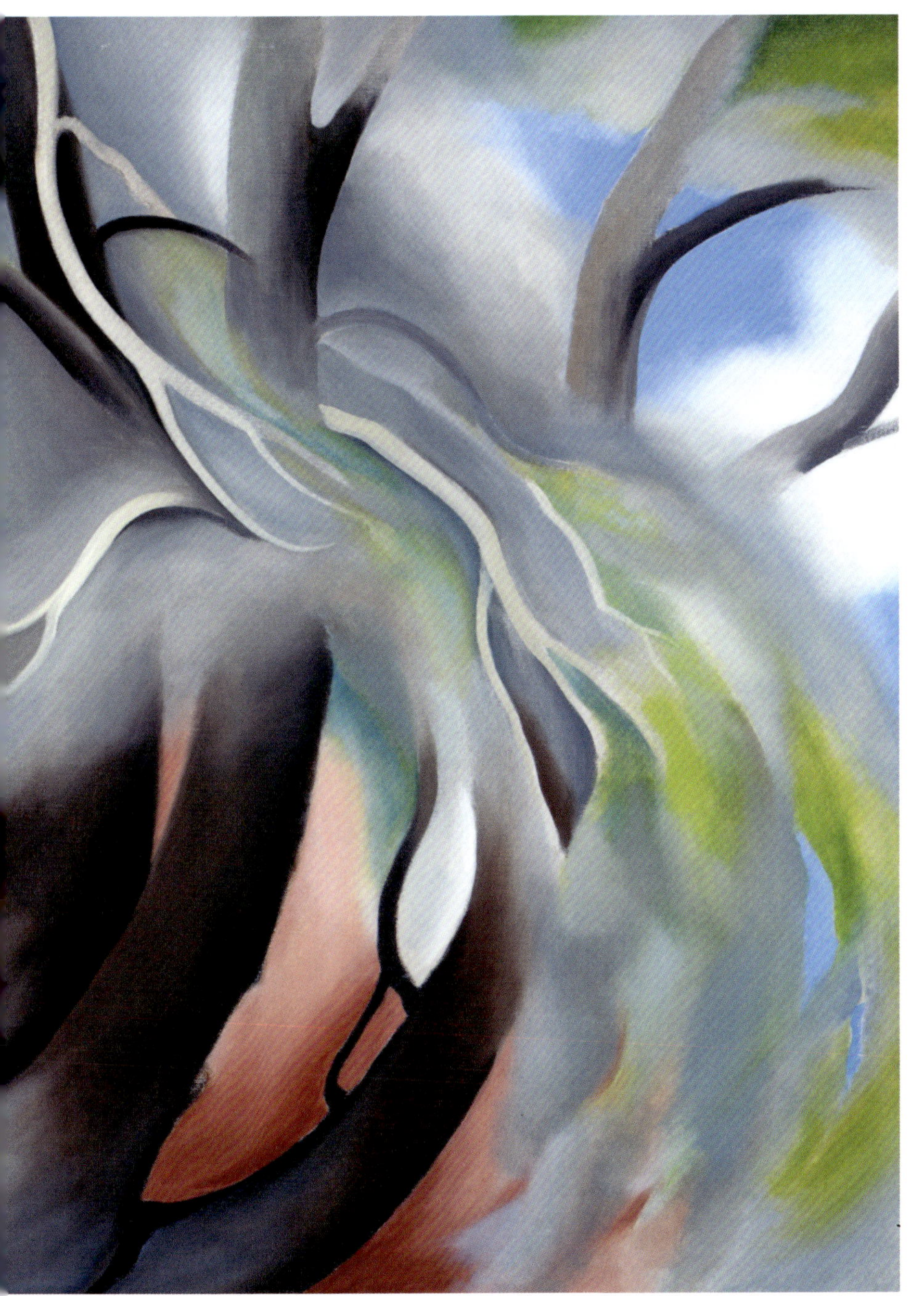

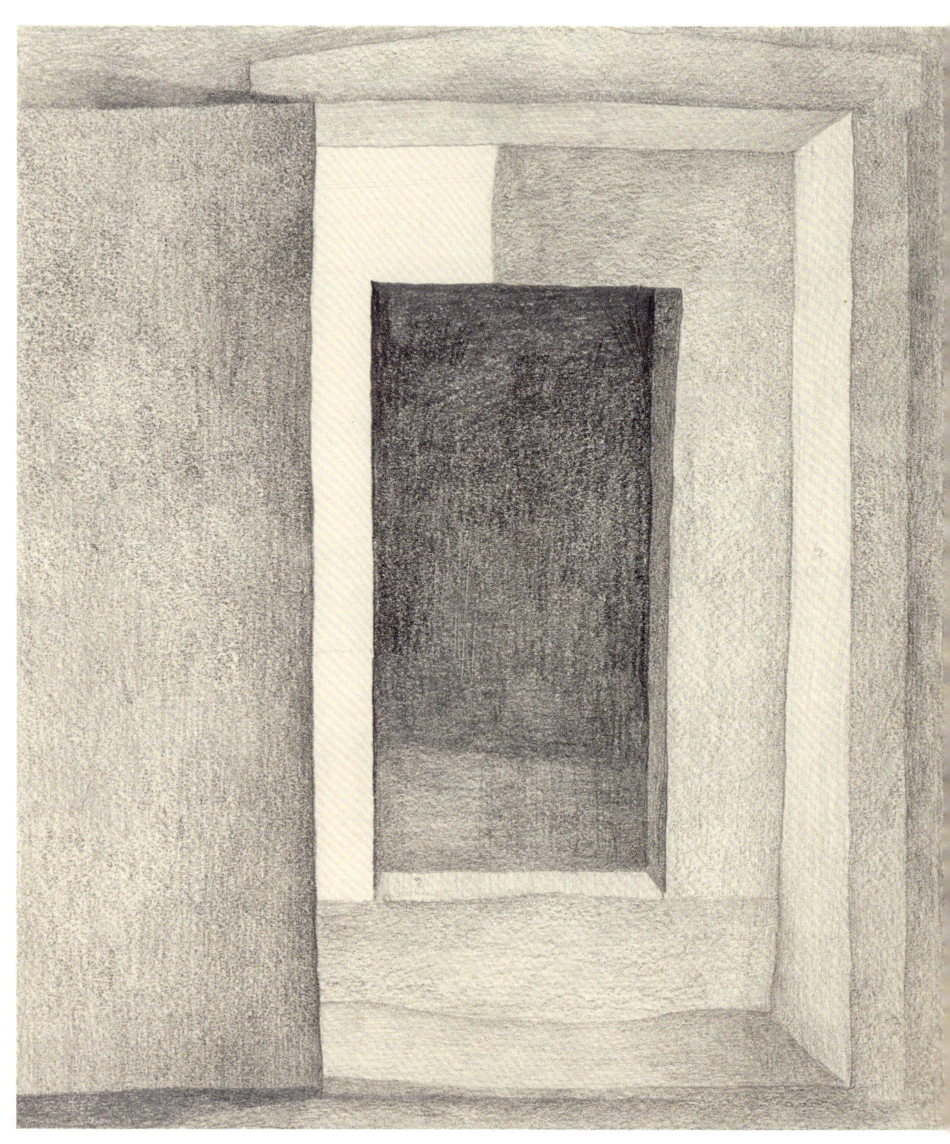

Untitled (Patio Door) c.1946
Graphite on paper
43.2 × 35.6

In the Patio I 1946
Oil paint on paper
76.2 × 60.9

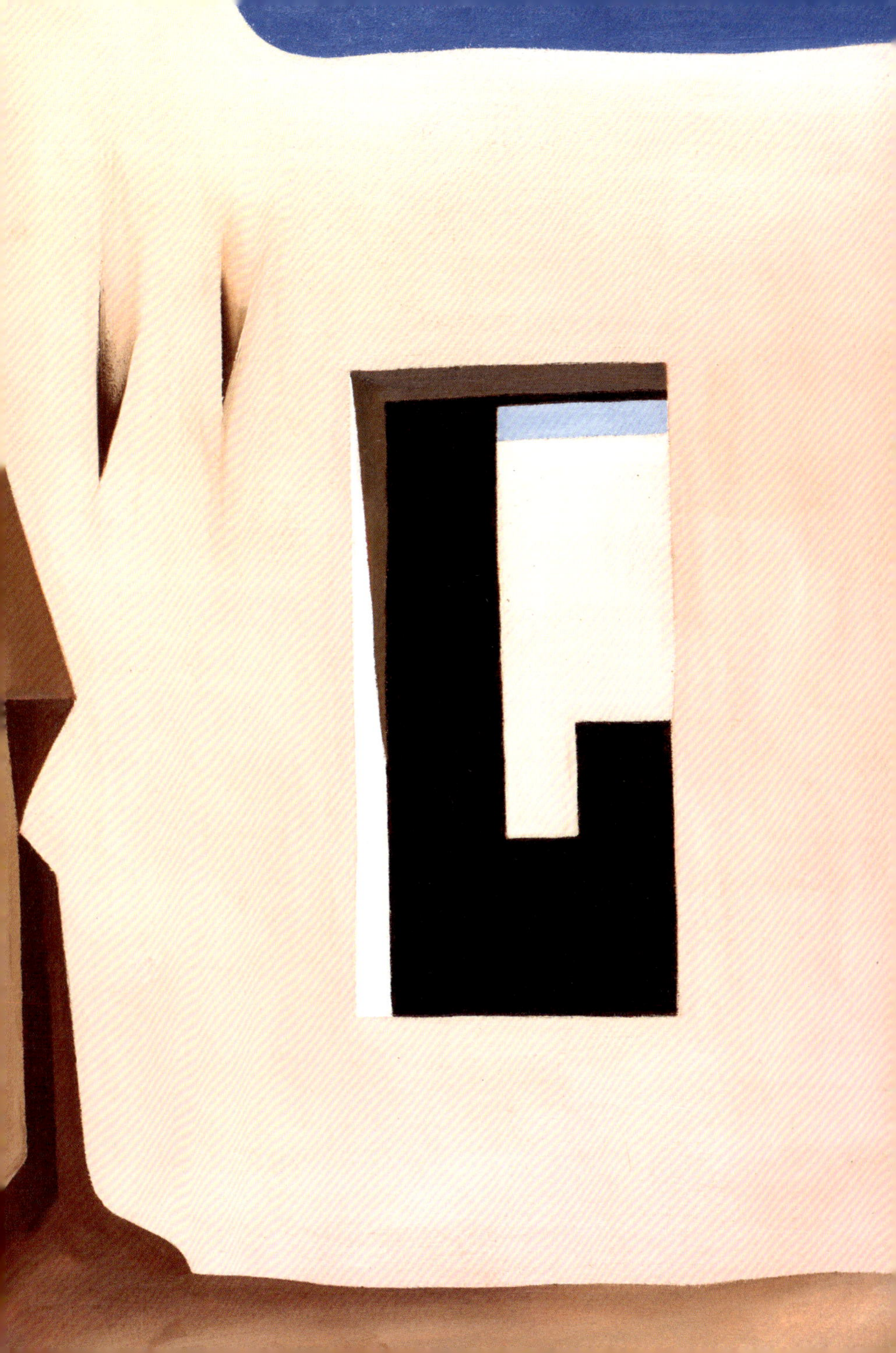

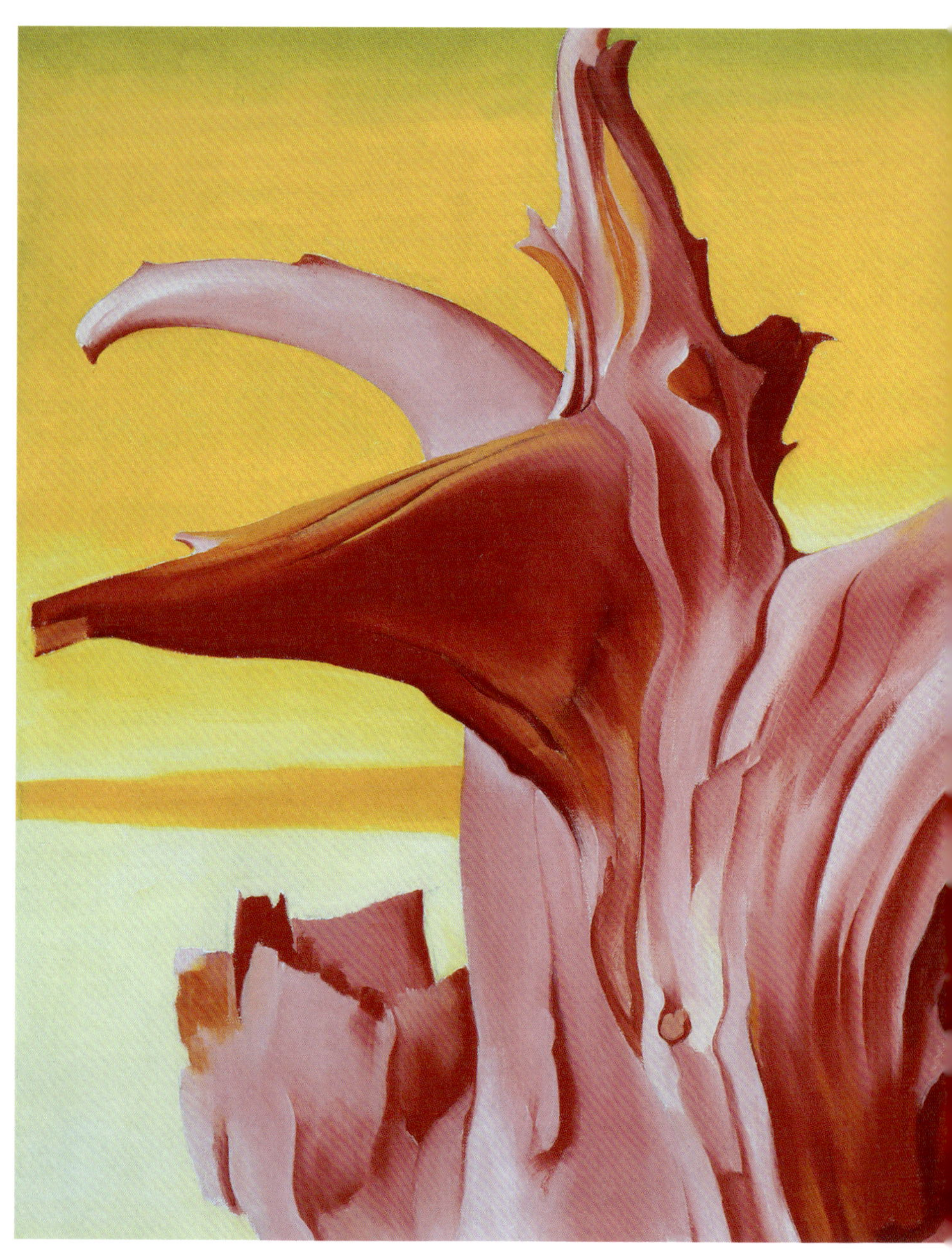

Red Tree, Yellow Sky 1952
Oil paint on canvas
76.2 × 121.3

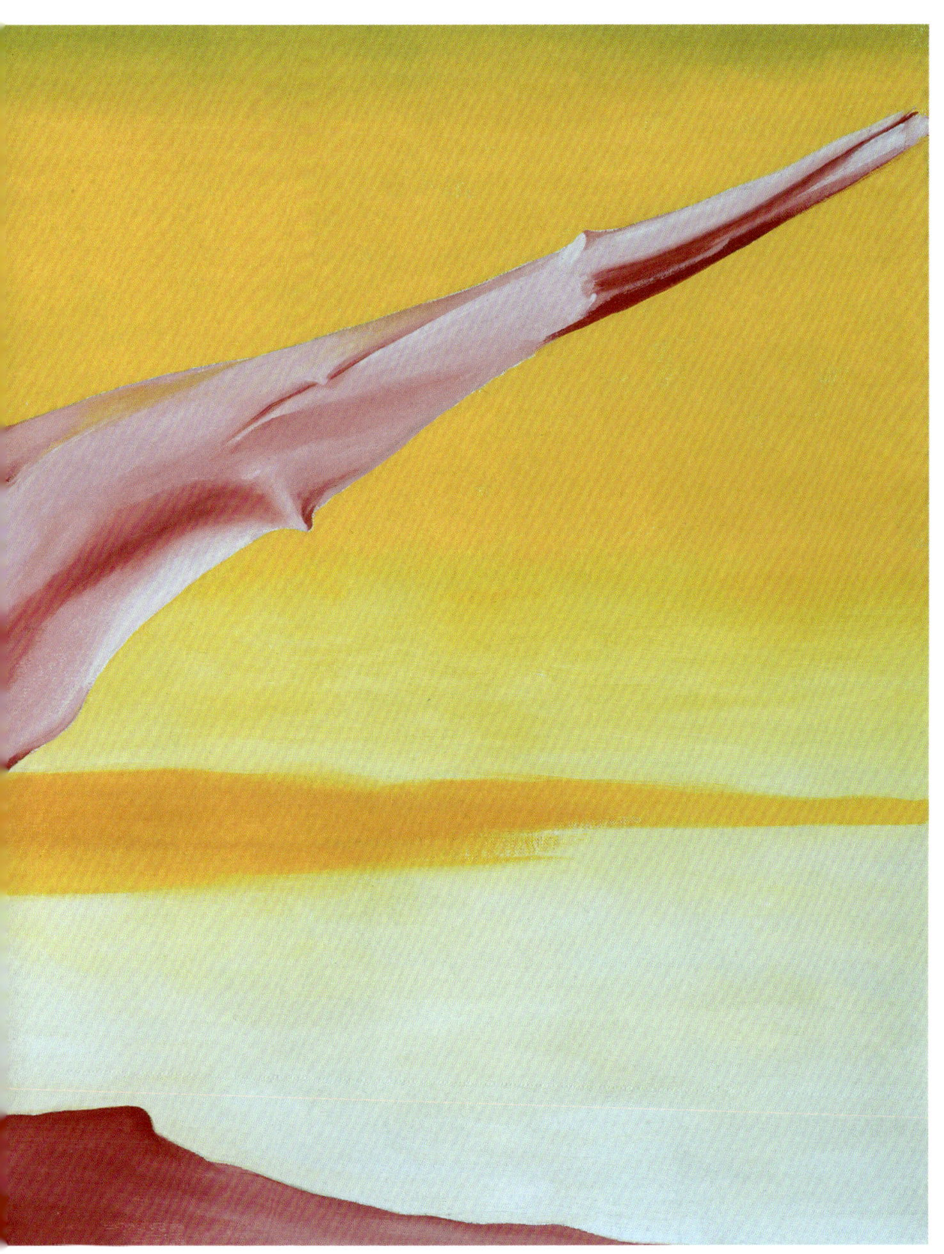

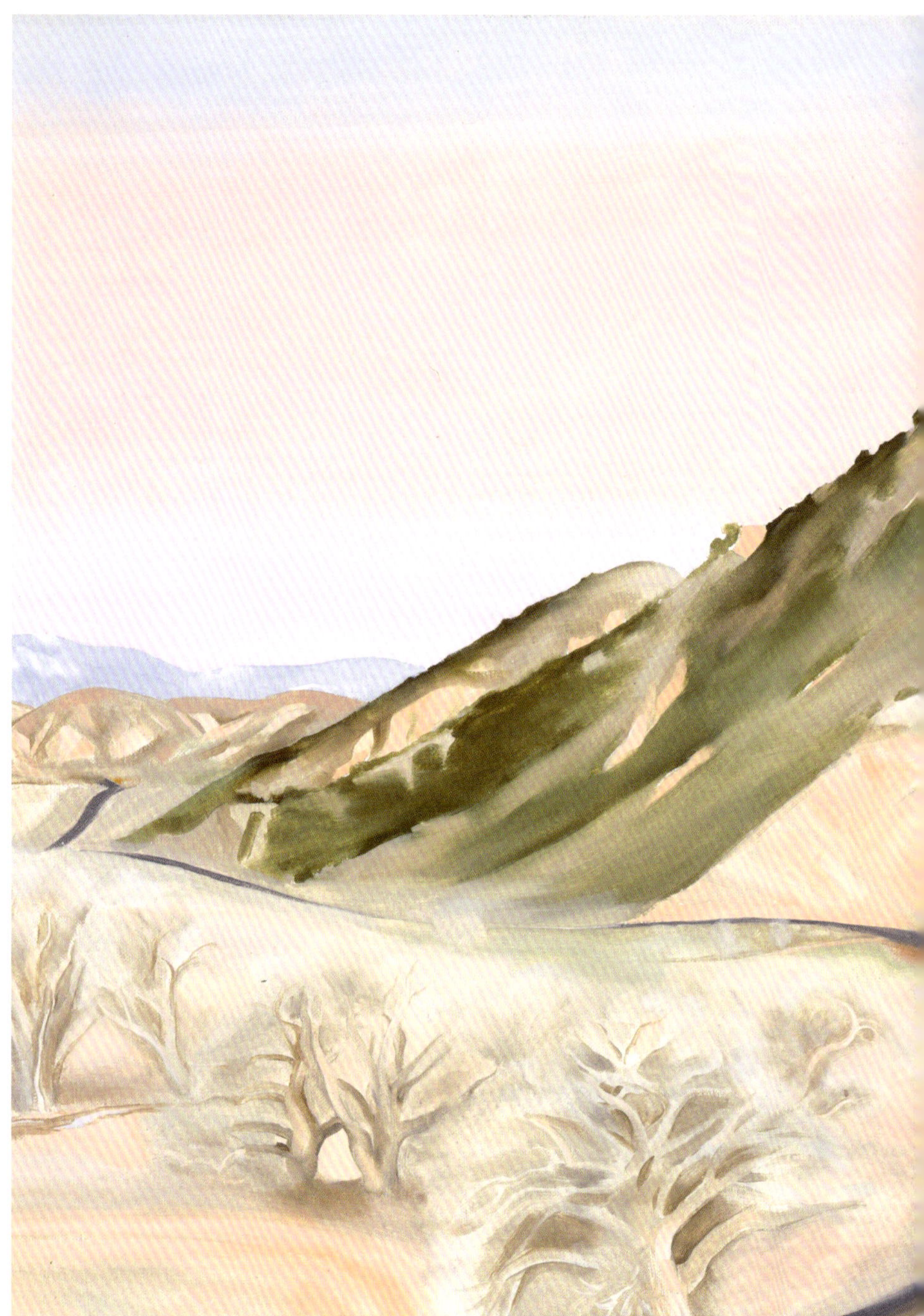

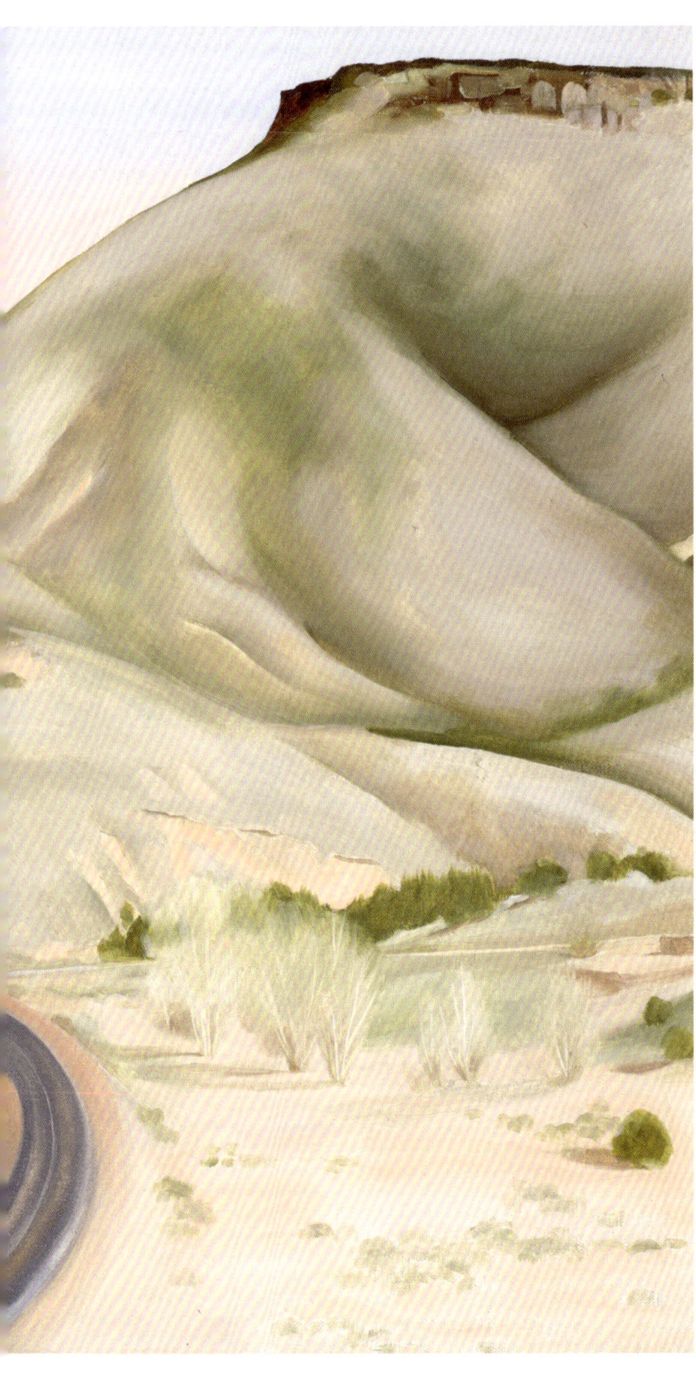

Mesa and Road East II 1952
Oil paint on canvas
66 × 91.9

Black Door with Red 1954
Oil paint on canvas
121.9 × 213.4

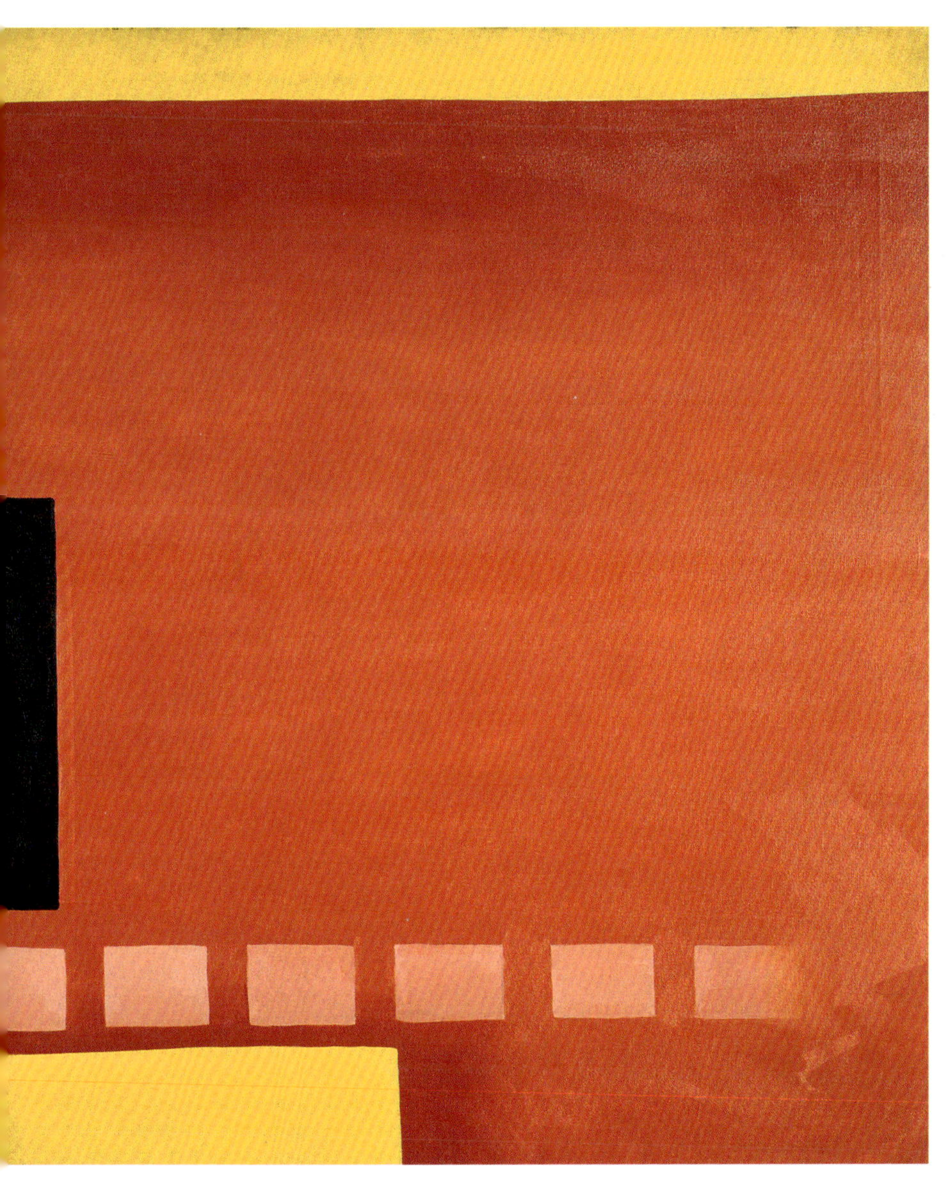

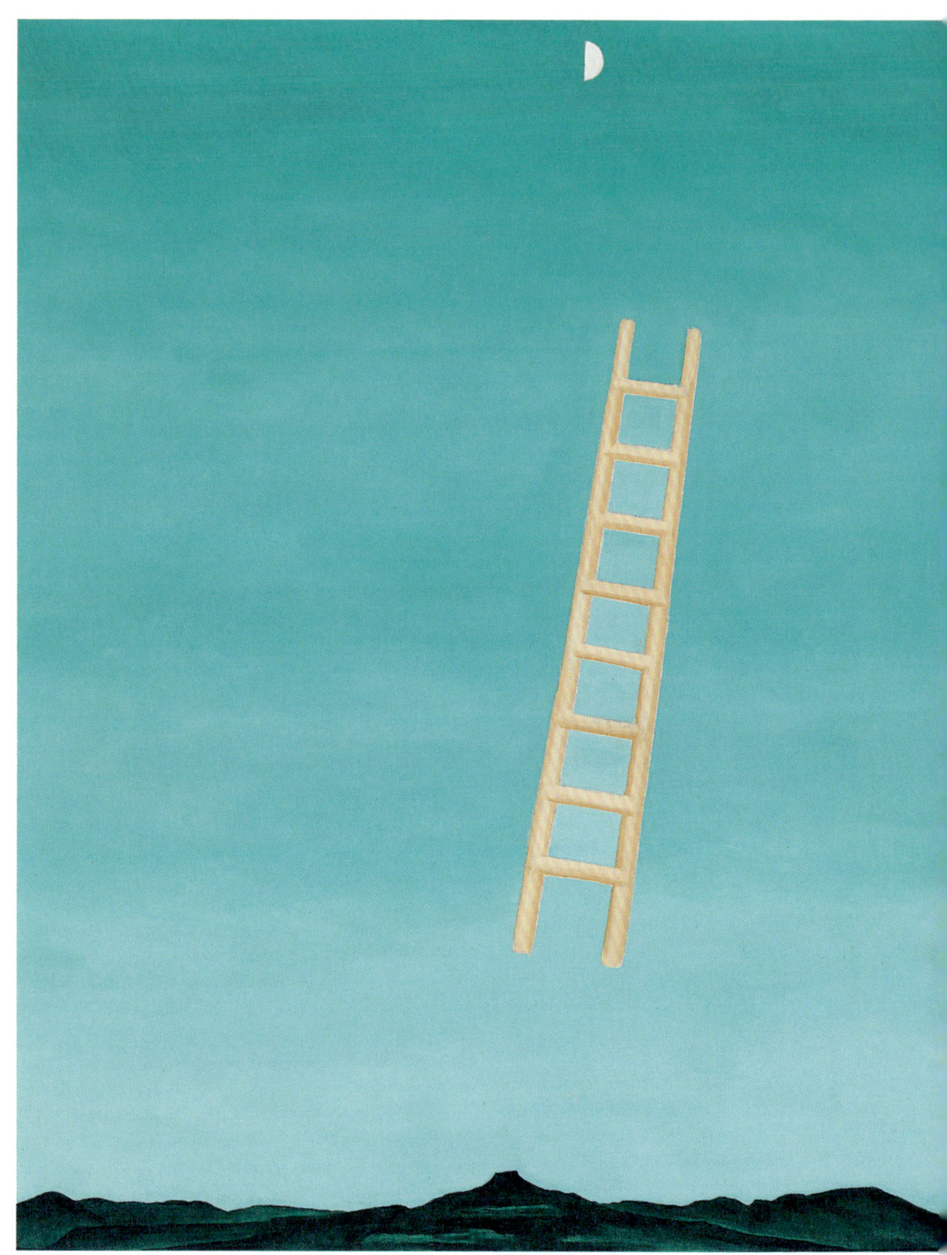

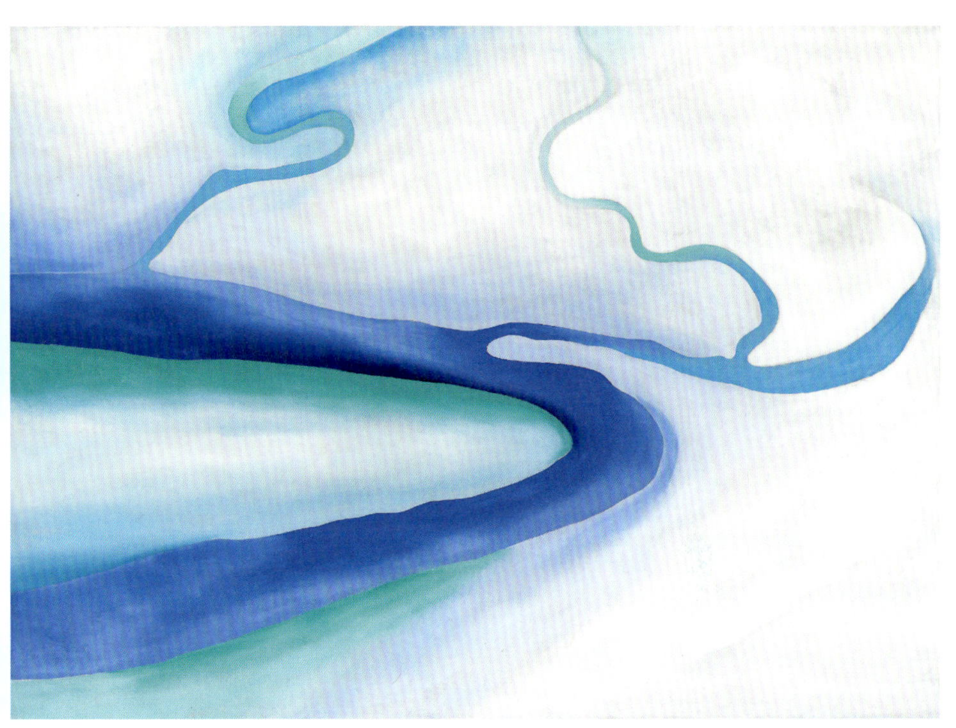

Ladder to the Moon 1958
Oil paint on canvas
102.1 × 76.8

It was Blue and Green 1960
Oil paint on canvas
76.3 × 101.6

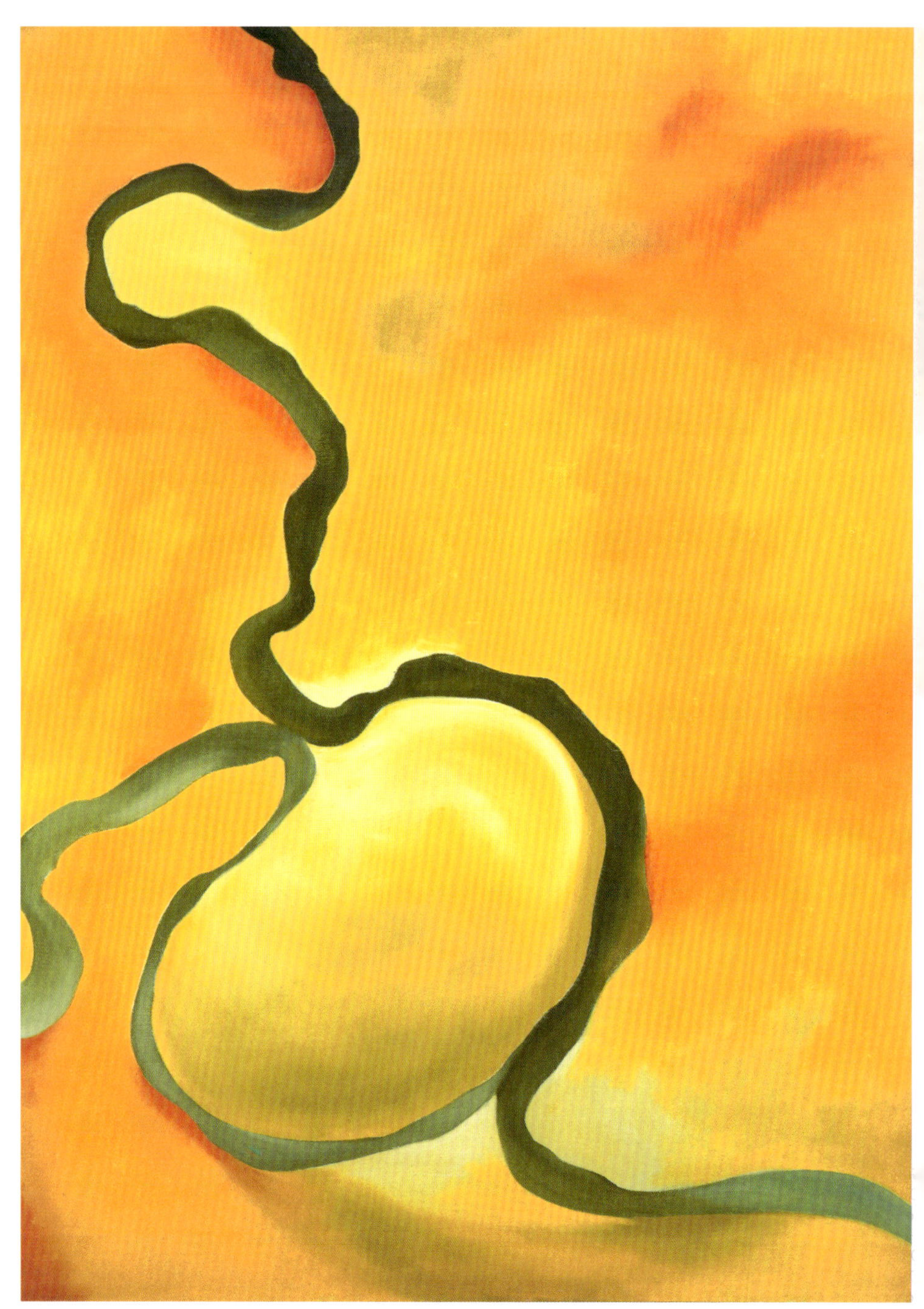

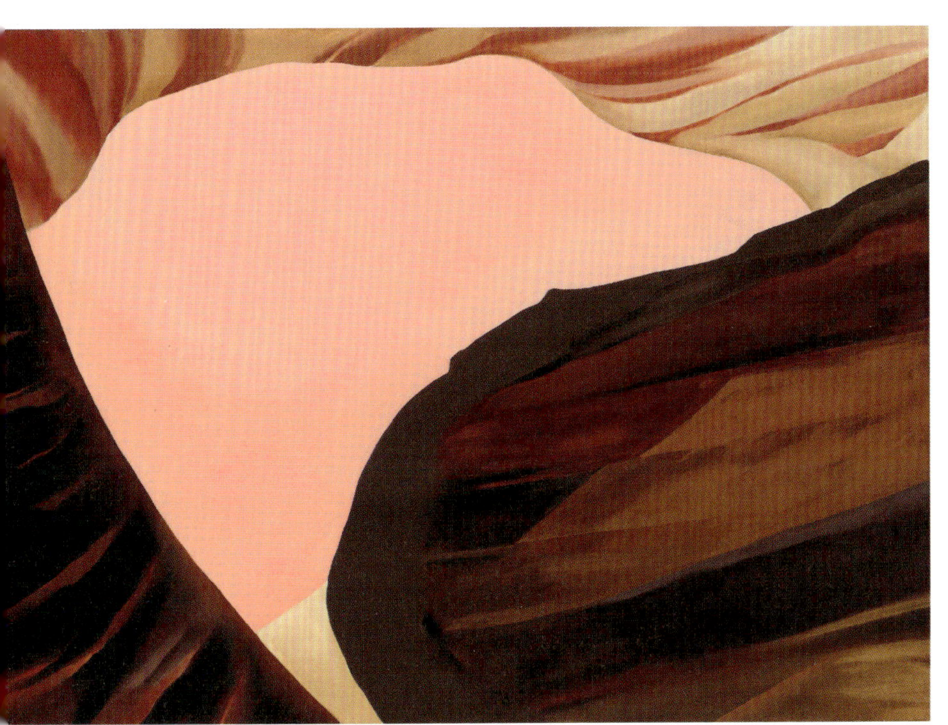

ìreen, Yellow and Orange 1960
Dil paint on canvas
:01.6 × 76.2

Dn the River I c.1965
Dil paint on canvas
02 × 76.9

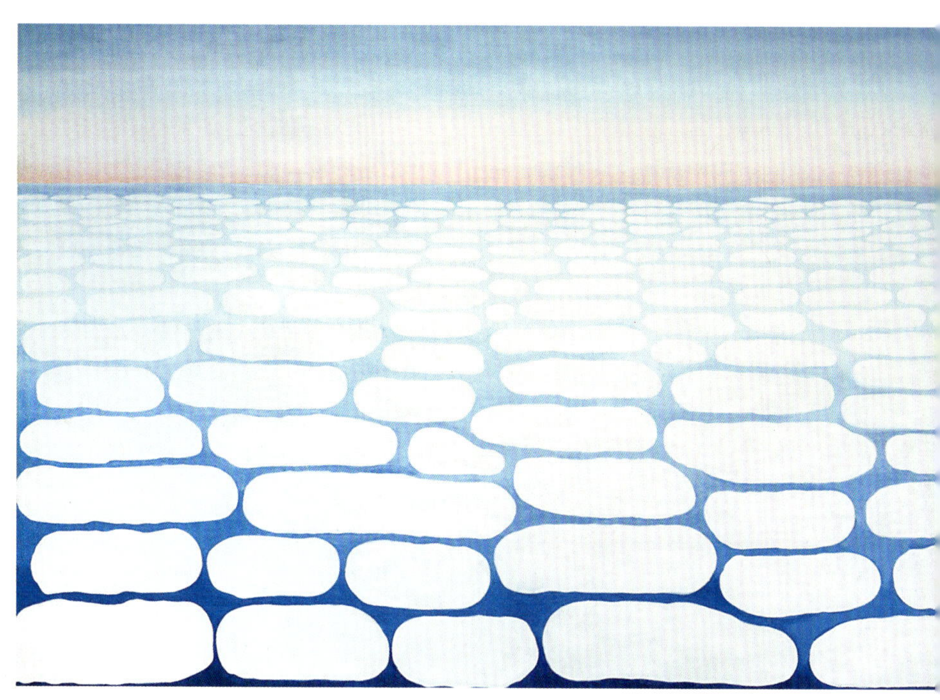

Sky Above Clouds IV 1965
Oil paint on canvas
243.8 × 731.5

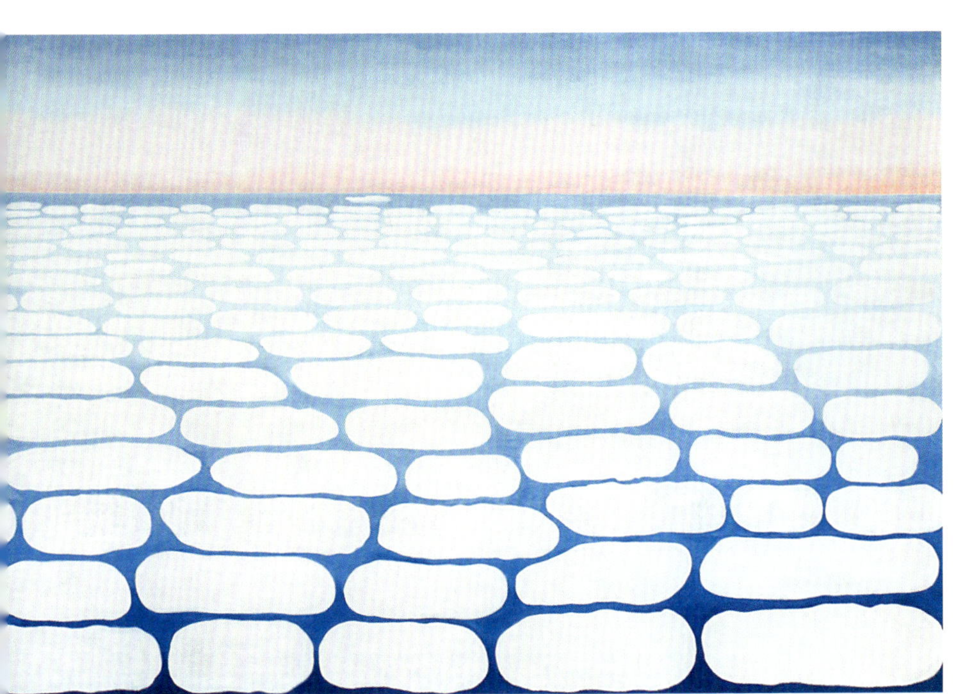

NOTES

1. O'Keeffe, letter to Sherwood Anderson, September 1923(?), in *Georgia O'Keeffe: Art and Letters*, exh. cat., National Gallery of Art, Washington 1987, p.174.

2. Critic William Murrell used the term 'inner harmony' to describe O'Keeffe's early work; see Nancy J. Scott, *Georgia O'Keeffe*, London 2015, p.67.

3. Roxana Robinson, *Georgia O'Keeffe: A Life*, London 1989, p.18.

4. Dow had studied in Paris in the 1880s, working closely with French artist Paul Gauguin and the Nabis who applied the aesthetic qualities of Japanese woodblock prints to their work.

5. O'Keeffe, letter to Anita Pollitzer, December 1915, in *Lovingly, Georgia: The Complete Correspondence of Georgia O'Keeffe and Anita Pollitzer*, ed. Clive Giboire, New York 1990, p.103.

6. In 1905 Stieglitz opened his first gallery, Little Galleries of the Photo-Secession, on 291 Fifth Avenue, New York. The space became commonly known as '291' and offered American audiences the chance to see modernist artworks by Paul Cézanne, Auguste Rodin and Henri Matisse among others, for the first time.

7. O'Keeffe, letter to Stieglitz, Charlottesville, 27 July 1916, in *Georgia O'Keeffe: Art and Letters*, p.154.

8. Sarah Greenough, 'Touching the Centre: Georgia O'Keeffe and Alfred Stieglitz's Artistic Dialogue', in *Georgia O'Keeffe*, exh. cat., Tate, London 2016, p.55.

9. O'Keeffe, letter to Pollitzer, June 1915, *Lovingly, Georgia*, p.5.

10. Stieglitz, letter to O'Keeffe, April 1917, *My Faraway One: Selected Letters of Georgia O'Keeffe and Alfred Stieglitz*, vol.1 1915–33, ed. Sarah Greenough, New Haven 2011, p.132.

11. Lisa Mintz Messinger, *Georgia O'Keeffe*, London 2001, p.50.

12. O'Keeffe, letter to Stieglitz, Canyon, Texas, 4 September 1916, in *Georgia O'Keeffe: Art and Letters*, p.155.

13. O'Keeffe, letter to Stieglitz, New Mexico, 15 August 1917, *My Faraway One*, vol.1, p.181.

14. O'Keeffe, letter to Anderson, Lake George, September 1923, in *Georgia O'Keeffe: Art and Letters*, p.173.

15. Messinger, *Georgia O'Keeffe*, p.79.

16. Griselda Pollock, 'Seeing O'Keeffe Seeing', in *Georgia O'Keeffe*, exh. cat., p.113.

17. O'Keeffe, letter to Russell Vernon Hunter, New York, 1932, *Georgia O'Keeffe: Art and Letters*, p.207.

18. O'Keeffe, letter to Stieglitz, 2 May 1929, *My Faraway One*, vol.1, p.413.

19. Ibid, p.525.

20. O'Keeffe, letter to Stieglitz, York Beach, Maine, 15 September 1926, *My Faraway One*, vol.1, p.373.

21. Lloyd Goodrich and Doris Bry (eds), *Georgia O'Keeffe*, exh. cat., Whitney Museum of American Art, New York 1970, p.23.

22. O'Keeffe, in *Georgia O'Keeffe*, a film by Perry Miller Adato, 1977, Thirteen /WNET.

23. O'Keeffe, *Some Memories of Drawings*, New York 1974, n.p.

24. The exhibition travelled to the Art Institute of Chicago and the San Francisco Museum of Art and gained extensive media coverage, catapulting O'Keeffe into a celebrity status previously unknown to the artist.

25. Doris Bry was O'Keeffe's close confidant and sole agent for over thirty years and helped organise countless exhibitions and edited several publications on the artist and her husband, Alfred Stieglitz.

CREDITS

COPYRIGHT

© The Art Institute of Chicago 66

© The Metropolitan Museum of Art 19, 28, 56, 60

© Milwaukee Museum 9

© Philadelphia Museum of Art 44

© Board of Trustees, National Gallery of Art, Washington 23

PHOTO CREDITS

Amon Carter Museum of American Art, Fort Worth, Texas, Purchase with assistance from the Anne Burnett Tandy Accessions Fund, 1995.8 cover, 37

The Art Institute of Chicago / Art Resource, NY / Scala, Florence 66, 70, 90–1

Museum of Fine Arts, Boston. All rights reserved / Scala, Florence 80–1

Brooklyn Museum, 87.136.3_SL1.jpg 88

Centre Pompidou, MNAM-CCI, Dist. GrandPalaisRmn / Bertrand Prévost 45

Christie's Images, London / Scala, Florence 68–9

Chrysler Museum of Art, Norfolk, Virginia Bequest of Walter P. Chrysler, JR. 89.63 84–5

Courtesy Crystal Bridges Museum of American Art, Bentonville, Arkansas. Photography by Dwight Primiano 32–3, 57

Cultural Archive / Alamy Stock Photo 4

Museum of Fine Arts, Houston / Museum purchase funded by the Agnes Cullen Arnold Endowment Fund / Bridgeman Images frontispiece

The Menil Collection, Houston, photo by Paul Hester 26

Image copyright The Metropolitan Museum of Art / Art Resource / Scala, Florence 19, 28, 34, 56, 60

Digital image, The Museum of Modern Art, New York/ Scala, Florence 50

Photo: Minneapolis Institute of Art 71

Minneapolis Institute of Art / Gift of funds from the Regis Corporation, Mr. and Mrs. W. John Driscoll, the Beim Foundation, the Larsen Fund, and by public subscription / Bridgeman Images 46

Photo Georgia O'Keeffe Museum, Santa Fe / Art Resource / Scala, Florence 12, 20, 27, 29, 30, 35, 36, 38, 39, 42, 48–9, 51, 58, 61, 67, 72–3, 74–5, 76–7, 78, 82–3, 89

Georgia O'Keeffe Museum, Santa Fe / Art Resource, NY 29, 30, 35, 38, 42, 58, 61, 64–5, 74–5, 78, 82–3, 89

The Phillips Collection, Washington, USA / Bridgeman Images 43

Photography by Edward C. Robison III 47

San Francisco Museum of Modern Art / Bridgeman Images 40–1

Digital image Whitney Museum of American Art / Licensed by Scala 10, 54–5, 59, 86, 87

Photo: Mark Woods 15

The publishers have made every effort to trace the copyright holders of the works illustrated in this book and apologise for any omissions or errors that may have been made.

INDEX

Page references in *italics* indicate images.

First published 2025 by order of the Tate Trustees
by Tate Publishing, a division of Tate Enterprises
Ltd Millbank, London SW1P 4RG
www.tate.org.uk

A catalogue record for this book is available from the British Library

ISBN 978 1 84976 974 7

Distributed in the United States and Canada by ABRAMS, New York

Library of Congress Control Number applied for

Commissioning Editor: Emma Poulter
Project Editor: Aki Gurung
Production: Juliette Dupire
Picture Research: Roz Hill
Designed by Astrid Stavro Studio
Colour reproduction by DL Imaging, London
Printed and bound in Italy by Printer Trento, S.r.l

Cover: Georgia O'Keeffe, *Series I – No.1* 1918 (see p.37)
Frontispiece: Georgia O'Keeffe, *Grey Lines with Black, Blue and Yellow* c.1923 (detail)
Oil paint on canvas, 121.9 × 76.2

Measurements of artworks are given in centimetres, height before width and depth

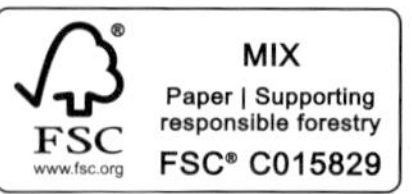

THE AUTHOR

Genevieve Barton is a curator and researcher based in London. She is currently Assistant Curator, International Art at Tate Modern where she works on exhibitions and displays, most recently co-curating *Expressionists: Kandinsky, Münter & The Blue Rider* (2024).